For Richard Paul

may your "ship" always
be tall, your course straight,
and your days happy.

Love — Happy Birthday
Your Mom

7-21-92

THE ROMANCE OF
TALL SHIPS

The British topsail schooner
'Sir Winston Churchill'
(left) being overhauled by
the huge Russian ship
'Sedov' at the start of the
1990 Tall Ships Race from
Plymouth, England to
Laconruna, Spain.

THE ROMANCE OF
TALL SHIPS

Jonathan Eastland

GALLERY BOOKS
An Imprint of W. H. Smith Publishers Inc.
112 Madison Avenue
New York City 10016

A QUINTET BOOK

produced for
GALLERY BOOKS
An imprint of W.H. Smith Publishers Inc.
112 Madison Avenue
New York, New York 10016

ISBN 0-8317-7461-4

This book was designed and produced by
Quintet Publishing Limited
6 Blundell Street
London N7 9BH

Creative Director: Terry Jeavons
Art Director: Ian Hunt
Designer: Stuart Walden, Wayne Blades
Project Editor: David Barraclough
Editor: Henrietta Wilkinson

Typeset in Great Britain by
Central Southern Typesetters, Eastbourne
Manufactured in Hong Kong by
Regent Publishing Services Limited
Printed in Hong Kong by
Leefung-Asco Printers Limited

DEDICATION

This work is dedicated to the memory of my
Grandfather, Herbert Harold Rose, Master,
S.S. Gloucester Castle, killed in action, 15th July
1942.

CONTENTS

Chapter One

AN ERA OF SAIL

The Legacy of the Clipper Ship

IN THE EARLY NINETEENTH CENTURY, when the idea of commercial steam-ships was still mostly a shipowner's dream on a designer's drawing board, the development of the fast sailing ship was in its infancy. The era of the China tea races between the great British and American clippers of the 1850s and 60s; the record passages from America's East Coast to the crazy gold rush stake-outs of California; and the Great Grain races from Australia to England were yet to come upon the world. Sailing ship design was still struggling to refine the lines of bulky packet ships and the Black-wall Frigate type much favoured by naval admirals of the day for their capacious troop- or passenger-carrying ability, long flush decks, great beam, bulging bows and massive scantlines. This type of design was a natural progression from the earlier short and dumpy vessels of the previous century, and they performed well, serving companies such as the East India Line until its demize in 1834, and for a further 20 years or more. But these were functional ships with a functional appearance. They lacked the grace and elegance of the next generation which were to come from ship builders of the likes of Donald McKay.

LEFT: *The clipper 'Cutty Sark' overhauls the White Star liner 'Britannic' in this reproduction of a painting by the artist David Cobb.*

*D*onald McKay hailed from Nova Scotia, Canada, and on arrival in New York became an apprentice in the shipyard of Isaac Webb. Webb's son William was to become, along with McKay and Samuel Hart Pook, one of the great American clipper ship designers. In 1840, McKay established his own shipyard in east Boston from where a number of record-breaking sailing ships were to slide down the tallow-greased launchways.

They included the *James Baines* and the *Sovereign of the Seas,* which both achieved speeds of more than 20 knots in a four hour period. McKay had a tendency to build each successive ship larger than her predecessor. The *Great Republic,* at 4,555 tons (4,628 t), was the largest wooden sailing ship ever built, but her strength and speed in a good blow were never tested; at the end of her first voyage from the yard in Boston to New York, she caught fire and was reduced to a hulk. McKay's most successful clippers were *Lightning, Champion of the Seas, James Baines* and *Donald McKay,* all launched between 1854 and 1855. They were built for British shipowner James Baines and employed in the Australian wool trade. *Champion of the Seas* laid claim

ABOVE: *Bostonian Donald McKay was one of the great clipper ship designers and builders of the nineteenth century.*

LEFT: *The British Royal Navy's 'HMS Volage' under sail during a voyage to the West Indies in 1895. This full rigged ship, one of the first iron-clads, was equipped with a steam engine but could make 18 knots under sail with her funnel down and propeller up.*

to the best day's run for a square rigged ship, sailing 467 nautical miles (over 750 kms) from noon to noon on 11–12 December, 1854, while on passage from Liverpool, England to Melbourne, Australia – an average speed of 19.4 knots. *Lightning* was 237½ ft (72 m) on the deck with a 44 ft (13.5 m) beam and displaced 2,084 tons (2,117 t). In 1856, her master recorded a seven day run of 2,188 nautical miles (over 3,500 kms), averaging 13 knots.

One hundred years since the heyday of these great ships, present-day ocean racing yacht technology is at last beginning to rival the high performance figures that some of the larger clippers were easily capable of. In terms of size, of course, there is no comparison; an 80 ft (24 m) racing yacht is a mere toy, a solitary scudding cloud, compared with the giant steel-built thunderheads of later years of the nineteenth century. But nevertheless, the comparison helps to realize the power of a great ship under sail, and how it must have felt to hurtle across the ocean.

In the recent Whitbread Round the World yacht race, a Spanish maxi yacht, *Fortuna Extra Lights,* of about 77 ft (23.4 m) overall and carrying 2,534 sq feet (773 sq m) of sail, made the longest noon to noon distance run of 394 nautical miles (over 630 kms) on the second leg of the race between Punte del Este in Uruguay and Fremantle in Western Australia; an average speed of 16.4 knots or nearly 19 mph (30.5 kmph) over a 24-hour period. But modern yachts are designed to surf in the huge wave patterns of the southern ocean, that 10 degree band of latitudes known to old timers as the 'roaring forties', from southern Africa to the south west tip of Australia. There were many occasions during this race when her skipper reported the speedometer 'off the clock' as the yacht raced from one wave crest to another at speeds of over 30 knots. Claims such as these seem as wild today as did those of clipper ship sailors whose masters drove their vessels so hard their lee rails would be awash for much of a long passage. High speeds under sail in a variety of hull shapes and sizes were certainly possible and are often close to those officially logged. Modern-day photographic records also help to support such claims.

The *Cutty Sark,* arguably the most famous survivor of the clipper ship era, was built in Dumbarton, Scotland by Scott & Linton in 1869 for a London shipowner. She measured 212 ft 5 in (64.7 m) on the deck with a beam of 36 ft (11 m), and displaced 1,330 tons (1,351 t) with a full cargo. The average length of many of her wooden predecessors was a mere 150 ft (46 m) overall – not much more than twice the size of the modern maxi yacht *Fortuna.* Built originally for the tea trade between England and China, the *Cutty Sark's* owner, Captain John 'White Hat' Willis (himself a sailing ship master who had inherited a sizeable fleet of ships from his father) nurtured high hopes that she would sail her passages faster than any ship then plying the route. However, *Thermopylae* was generally considered the fastest clipper afloat at the height of the China tea trade.

During her maiden voyage in 1870, *Cutty Sark* sailed from Shanghai on 25 June and passed off Beachy Head on the Sussex coast of England on 12 October, 109 days later. This was not notably faster than her rivals on the same route, and some of those who commanded her during the seven years she ran the China coast thought her slow. Others argued that she was a fine sailing vessel, which rarely lost way even in light winds. The average speed for a China tea clipper for the whole voyage was about 6.5 knots; the *Cutty Sark* averaged 8.

THE CUTTY SARK

THE OPENING OF THE SUEZ CANAL on 17th November 1869 effectively marked the demise of the China clipper tea trade; the route through the Mediterranean to the Far East eventually enabled steamships to cut the voyage time from London to Shanghai by half. The *Cutty Sark* was kept in the tea trade from the time of her launch and completed eight round voyages:

YEAR	FROM	TO	PASSAGE
1870	Shanghai	Beachy Head (Sussex)	109 days
1871	Shanghai	North Foreland	107 days
1872	Shanghai	Portland Bill	120 days
1873	Shanghai	Deal (Kent)	116 days
1874	Woosung	Deal (Kent)	118 days
1875	Woosung	Deal (Kent)	122 days
1876	Woosung	Start Point	108 days
1877	Woosung	Scilly Isles	122 days

Her average cargo for these voyages was about 591 tons (603 t) of tea carried in chests.

After a period of five years spent tramping, the *Cutty Sark* was employed again in regular sailings on the Australian wool trade. These are the passages she made:

YEAR	FROM	TO	PASSAGE
1883–84	Newcastle, NSW	Deal	82 days
1884–85	Newcastle, NSW	Dock	80 days
1885	Sydney, NSW	Downs	73 days
1887	Sydney, NSW	Lizard	70 days
1887–88	Newcastle, NSW	Lizard	69 days
1888–89	Sydney, NSW	London	86 days
1889–90	Sydney, NSW	London	75 days
1890–91	Sydney, NSW	London	93 days
1891–92	Sydney, NSW	Lizard	83 days
1893	Sydney, NSW	Bishop's Rock	90 days
1893–94	Sydney, NSW	Hull	93 days
1894–95	Brisbane	London	84 days

On her last voyage of this period she loaded 5,304 bales of wool, the most she had ever carried.

ABOVE: *The four masted barque 'Peking' was typical of the big ships owned by Ferdinand and Carl Laeisz who operated the 'Flying P' line of windjammers from Europe to South America.*

In 1872, she was loading tea in Shanghai for her third voyage home at the same time as the *Thermopylae* loaded a similar cargo; the latter was the larger vessel at 1,300 tons (1,321 t) gross. During the passage home, the *Cutty Sark* achieved noon to noon runs of 320, 327 and 340 nautical miles (512, 523 and 544 km), slightly more than 13–14 knots. But she still failed to prove herself against the Aberdeen clipper; for while leading the *Thermopylae* by some 400 miles (640 km) in the Indian Ocean and sailing hard in heavy weather, she lost her rudder and landed her cargo in London a week behind her rival. Six years earlier, a 16 vessel race out of Pagoda Anchorage on China's Min River had resulted in a nail-biting finish between the clippers *Ariel* and *Taeping* when, after racing across 15,000 miles (24,000 km) of ocean, the two finished the race off Gravesend only one mile (1.6 km) apart.

In the ensuing years, the *Cutty Sark* underwent a sail surgery. Her rig was cut down

and she searched the world for a miscellany of cargoes from Wales to Japan, from China and back to Australia, the Philippines and the East Coast of North America. In 1885, Captain Richard Woodget, a celebrated sailing ship master with a reputation for hard driving, took command of the ship while she was engaged in the wool trade between Australia and England. Under his command, Woodget gradually improved the vessel's passage times from 82 days, while under Captain E Moore, down to 69 days in 1888, on a run from Newcastle NSW, Australia to the Lizard in Cornwall, England.

The number of wool bales crammed into the ship's hold increased with each voyage – Woodget's owners must have been pleased. It is astounding that even at 25 years old, the *Cutty Sark* was still overhauling larger, more modern and supposedly faster vessels. Her best ever recorded speed was 17.5 knots. During her last voyage under the British red ensign, with Woodget in command, she was homeward bound from Brisbane, Australia, with 5,304 bales of wool when she came upon the White Star Line's *California*, a four masted barque of nearly 3,000 tons (3,048 t), carrying wheat from California, US, to Liverpool, England.

Woodget noted in his logbook on 28 February, 1895, that the *California* was passed just south of the Equator, a gentle easterly breeze blowing at the time. As the *Cutty Sark* headed north for the English Channel a number of big ships were overhauled, with only the *California* hanging on until she too was beaten to port by 48 hours.

Shortly afterwards, the tea clipper began a new life under the Portuguese flag, sailing with the name of *Ferreira* under JA Ferreira and as *Maria do Amparo* until 1922. She had many adventurous voyages, including being caught in a hurricane in the West Indies when she dragged ashore and lost her rudder. Later she lay for several years in the lower reaches of London's River Thames at Greenhithe as a school ship, before finally being turned into a British national shrine at Greenwich, London.

To sailing ship lovers worldwide, the *Cutty Sark* remains both unique and beautiful, perhaps even the epitome of man's quest for speed, grace and power at sea in the commercial age of sail. Her designer, Hercules Linton, and his partner, the builder William Dundas Scott-Moncrieff, got only one thing wrong when calculating their figures – the cost of turning Willis's dream into reality. At £17 ($34) a ton, they under-quoted and went bankrupt. The *Cutty Sark* was finished by William Denny and Bros. of Leven.

But the story of the 'tall ship', as the English Poet Laureate John Masefield called these great sailing vessels, did not begin, and nor did it end, with that famous tea clipper. For centuries prior to the launch of the *Cutty Sark*, man had endeavoured to perfect the sailing ship and harness the power of the wind. Designs progressed from short, rounded, tubby hulls capable of slow, plodding voyages to the long and narrow elegance of the clippers. But the cargo capacity of clippers in the burgeoning decades of the Industrial Revolution was severely restricted by their construction. Most were built of planked timber; some, like the *Cutty Sark*, were of composite construction using transverse frames of best Lowmoor iron onto which the wood planks were secured. It was a form of construction much admired by naval architects well into the twentieth century and a number of large ocean racing and cruising yachts designed and built with composite hulls in the 1920s and 1930s are afloat today. Even so, there was an engineering limit to the size that a hull could be built in this fashion, Donald McKay's attempts with the *Great Republic* notwithstanding.

In the search for larger vessels, first iron and then steel were the primary building materials. Both were stronger than timber, and less prone to the huge hull deflections which would have arisen in a hull of comparative size built of wood. Designs changed too, from the fair and round bilged clippers, with their fine, convex forward entry and tapering stern lines, to more slab-sided, flat-bottomed vessels. These were merchant ships with a vengeance; floating warehouses capable of carrying huge cargoes of ore, wool, coal, nitrates, wheat and the hundreds of thousands of tons of other products desperately needed in a rapidly-expanding Europe and North America.

Masts and yards now had to be made of steel too, some with a diameter of at least 3 ft (1 m) at the heel, towering 177–196 ft (54–60 m) above the waterline. The main yard, the one carrying the largest sail, could be as much as 98 ft (30 m) end to end across the ship. The mainsail alone, the main driving force behind the ship, might weigh as much as a ton (1.016 t) – dry! And when it was sodden, it weighed a great deal more. All the standing and running rigging on these new goliaths was made of wire rope, their tail ends being spliced onto lengths of manilla so crews could avoid having their hands razored to shreds by minute wire strands which invariably split and curled off the rope. Laid in a line, all the rigging on a great sailing ship would stretch for miles. Big ones, those over 2,500 tons (2,540 t) gross, carried as many as 35 separate sails, over 40,000 sq ft (approximately 1 acre or .5 ha) of canvas. In a good breeze, average speeds of 13 knots were easily and frequently attained; often they sailed faster. In the heyday of the great windjammer (as they came to be called by steamship captains who could not catch them), 16–20 knots was not uncommon.

Most of the clipper ships had long, flush

BELOW: *The 1,034 ton (1,050 t) barquentine 'Renfield' was still trading in 1905 and is seen here moored in Ostend, Holland, awaiting cargo.*

LEFT: *'Falls of Halladale' inward bound with a full cargo under tow on the River Avon, England. Built in 1886 for the Scottish Falls line of Glasgow, this was a typical 'warehouse' ship grossing 2,026 tons (2,058 t).*

decks and a slightly raised after-deck at the stern, the poop, which covered the master's and officers' accommodation below it. The ship's wheel was fixed on the poop deck and in a gale the helm often required two men or more to turn the spokes and keep the ship on track. When a freak wave broke over the stern of the ship in a following sea, the chances of survival for the helmsmen and officers on watch were slim – and sometimes for the ship too. The expression 'to be pooped' came from this not infrequent happening.

As the designs for windjammers improved, shipowners listened more readily to their captain's advice. On many ships, a midships deckhouse was built spanning the beam of the ship. Both officers and men were accommodated here, next to the galley and below the navigating bridge which now housed the steering gear. It was a safer place to be in bad weather, the 'centre-castle' helping to break up the hundreds of tons of sea water which frequently flooded the main deck when driving the ship in heavy weather. Fore and aft, a raised cat-walk, called a 'flying bridge', linked the fo'c'sle head and the poop deck to the midships section; and in really bad weather, extra netting and lifelines would be rigged on the maindeck to ensure

that the men stayed on board when waves washed down the decks. Whereas the clipper ships often sailed with a crew of 35–40 men, these new windjammers could manage with less. The average was about 30, but in some cases, as modern technology in the form of bracing and halyard winches became commonplace, the complements were reduced still further.

Even as steam sounded the death knell for the sailing ship in the late 1890s, there were still thousands of windjammers sailing the oceans in search of cargoes and fast voyages. Some shipowners and owner/skippers refused to believe that steam would cause their great billowing ships to disappear off the face of the earth. And not unreasonably. A sailing ship could stay at sea longer than its steam counterpart as it needed no fuel – wind was free; they were less prone to the damage caused to funnels and superstructures by breaking seas, which could squash a steel plate flat in seconds; and it cost little to keep a windjammer anchored off a port while waiting for a cargo. Steamships, however, were expensive, smoky and, until the advent of the steam turbine in merchant ships, infernally slow.

Such was the optimism of the board of directors of the Laeisz Shipping Company of Hamburg – the 'Flying P' line – that they ordered the largest steel-hulled sailing vessel ever built by the JC Tecklenborg shipyard. The *Preussen* was a five-masted, full-rigged ship, built of steel and launched in 1902. She displaced 11,150 tons (11,328 t) and measured 440 ft (134 m) from stem to stern. Her beam was 54 ft (16 m) and she had a depth of 32½ ft (10 m) from keel to deck. A crew of 45 men was needed to man her maze of rigging and climb the dizzy heights of her masts, her main towering 224 ft (68 m) above the keel. She could set nearly 60,000 sq ft (18,300 sq m) of canvas, equal to approximately 6,000 brake horse power (4,476 KW). In good conditions she could make 17 knots; in the South Atlantic in 1903, her average for a 24-hour run of 368 miles (589 km) was 15.3 knots.

The *Preussen* might have stayed the course and shown a healthy profit for her owners in spite of steam (she could, after all, shake off some of the best tramp and early passenger steamers even in a moderate breeze), but a stroke of bad luck put an end to all that when she was outward bound for Chile, loaded with pianos. The steamer *Brighton*, thinking she could outsmart the great windjammer, tried to slip across her bows in the English Channel, but her skipper had badly misjudged the speed of the *Preussen*. When the collision took place, the mighty windjammer's foresails and bowsprit were carried away. She headed for harbour, her bows badly damaged, but without those headsails she was almost uncontrollable. The next day, she fetched up on rocks under Dover Cliffs off England's south coast and was never salvaged to sail again.

Many of the great sailing ships remembered today come from between the 1870s until well into the twentieth century. Gustaf Erikson, a Finn and the last great sailing shipowner, kept a fleet of 20 sailing ships at Mariehamn, on the island of Aland in the Baltic, in almost perfect trim until the mid 1940s. One remains, a floating museum and permanent reminder of the man's stubbornness in the face of new technology.

Herzogin Cecile, Preussen, Potosi, Priwall, Moshulu, Falls of Halladale, Granite State and *Cromdale* – just a handful of the wonderful names given to these ocean wanderers. Hundreds foundered in storms while navigating deep oceans: the notorious Cape Horn could suddenly turn calm into a devastating, screaming gale in minutes; and rock-strewn coasts around the British Isles (Devon, Cornwall and the Scilly Isles) and America (from California to Alaska) all became graveyards for some of the finest ships.

In the 1920s there were still a number of these great windjammers plying the seas, but the harbour walls of Australia's Newcastle, NSW, and the anchorage at Iquique off the South American coast were by then denuded of the forests of masts which would have greeted the sailor on arrival there only 20 years before. The opening of Ferdinand de Lessep's Suez Canal halved the time of a steamship voyage to the Antipodes or the Orient via the Cape of Good Hope. But small brigs, barquentines, schooners and sailing barges still plied their trade around Europe and up and down the eastern seaboard of North America until they too were gradually ousted by larger and faster steamships.

Today, the legacy of that great era of sail can be seen in the ships that have been lovingly restored to their former splendour. They form the backbone of the floating museums scattered worldwide, from New York to Honolulu, London to Mariehamn, Hamburg to San Diego, and on to Sydney. Some are still sailing alongside newer vessels, built for the purpose of training naval cadets and to give youngsters a chance to enjoy the sailing experience of a lifetime.

Many countries, governments, private individuals, syndicates and sail training associations are the owners of these latter day windjammers. Those which are not nationally owned and managed are kept afloat and in top condition by sponsorship, through donations from industry, and with the unstinting help of many volunteer workers whose only dream is to see these great ships restored. In recent years, the public

LEFT: *A forest of masts and rigging at rest in Plymouth's Milbay docks on the south coast of England evokes memories of a past era when ports were full of sailing ships.*

has shown an enthusiasm for the sea which has hitherto been untapped. Television and drama series such as *The Onedin Line* fuelled that enthusiasm. The famous *Cutty Sark Whisky* sponsored 'Tall Ship' races in association with the British Sail Training Association (STA), starting from ports all over the world, have helped to encourage entrepreneurs to restore long-forgotten hulks which sooner or later would have been lost in the sands of time. That many of these restored classics are sailing again at all is quite remarkable considering their age; that they are able to sail across the oceans they once traversed in search of a rich cargo crewed only by youngsters in search of adventure is astounding.

These fleets of training ships, as they are now mostly called, are comprized not only of older tonnage but also of the new windjammers. Fitted out with lightweight terylene sails, electric winches and a host of modern electronic navigational aids, they are easier to sail by far than their predecessors. Shipowners and captains of the last century would have given their eye-teeth to have been able to equip their vessels with today's technology. Had sail outsailed steam, who knows what we would be looking at today in terms of the flying windjammer.

There are those who would love to see the sailing ship return as a primary means of cargo transportation – and they are not just the environmentalists dedicated to the cause of outlawing fossil fuels. Industrialists who know that oil is their most expensive overhead in operating large, fast tankers and container ships, and tour operators who recognize the demand for romantic adventures have long been looking at ways to combine the best of both worlds. Modern sailing ships using the technology of ocean yacht racing and the aircraft industry are now a reality, sailing both for pleasure and profit. In years to come, the sail-powered ocean cruise liner is a predictable certainty. One or two have already been launched, proving a great success in the luxury tourist markets of North America, the Pacific and the Mediterranean. For the foreseeable future at least, it is unlikely that these hybrid vessels will return to the magnificent designs of the past; too many compromises need to be made in the way of size, accommodation and the size of machinery which shipowners still insist on installing. Nevertheless, naval architects with a bent towards wind power have produced designs that are just as exciting as their forbears. It is only a matter of time before the first one is built.

Chapter Two

SAILING SHIPS OF THE WORLD

IN THE SUMMER OF 1989, more than 100 tall ships gathered in the Port of London for a week before the start of the Cutty Sark Tall Ships race; in Rouen in France, over 50 more moored on the River Seine in the heartland of Normandy to help celebrate the country's Bicentennial anniversary. The oldest of these illustrious vessels was the 'Belem' which had been built in 1896 and which, after a varied career on merchant routes across the South Atlantic and several years under different flags as a private yacht, was eventually purchased by the Belem Foundation based in Paris and restored to her former glory.

Few windjammers from the nineteenth century survive today, either as floating museums or sailing ships in commission, but a number of vessels constructed in the earlier decades of this century are very much alive and well, lavishly maintained by various navies for the training of young sailors.

LEFT: *Pulling gigs hang in davits off the maindeck of the Italian sail training ship 'Amerigo Vespucci' in this dawn picture of square riggers moored at Rouen.*

The list below gives an idea of just how many square rigged sailing ships are in commission today.

SQUARE RIGGED SAILING SHIPS				
NAME	TYPE	YEAR	LENGTH*	COUNTRY
Alexander Von Humboldt	Barque	1906	206½ (63)	W. Germany
Amerigo Vespucci	Ship	1931	331 (101)	Italy
Asgard II	Brigantine	1981	108 (33)	Eire
Astrid	Brig	1918	141 (43)	UK
Belem	Barque	1896	190 (58)	France
Capitan Miranda	Ship	1930	197½ (60.2)	Uruguay
Christian Radich	Ship	1937	240 (73.15)	Denmark
Cuauhtemoc	Ship	1982	297 (90.5)	Mexico
Dar Mlodziezy	Ship	1981	357½ (109)	Poland
Druzhba	Ship	1987	357½ (109)	USSR
Eagle	Barque	1936	295 (90)	US
Gloria	Barque	1968	249 (76)	Colombia
Gorch Fock	Barque	1958	293 (89.3)	W. Germany
Henryk Rutkowski	Brigantine	1944	100 (30)	Poland
Iskra	Barquentine	1982	157½ (48)	Poland
Kaliakra	Barquentine	1984	160 (49)	Bulgaria
Kaskelot	Barque	1949	164 (50)	UK
Kruzenshtern	Barque	1926	380½ (116)	USSR
Libertad	Ship	1956	338 (103)	Argentina
Lord Nelson	Barque	1985	161 (49)	UK
Malcolm Miller	Topsail schooner	1968	157½ (48)	UK
Mir	Ship	1987	361 (110)	USSR
Sagres II	Barque	1937	293 (89.3)	Portugal
Sedov	Barque	1921	397 (121)	USSR
Shabab Oman	Schooner	1971	171 (52.1)	Oman
Simon Bolivar	Barque	1979	270 (82.3)	Venezuela
Sir Winston Churchill	Topsail schooner	1966	157½ (48)	UK
Sorlandet	Ship	1927	216 (65.8)	Norway
Statsraad Lehmkuhl	Barque	1914	321½ (98)	Norway

The measurements for the length of the vessel are given first in feet, then metres in brackets

ABOVE : *A quartermaster at the huge triple wheel of the West German training ship 'Gorch Fock'. In the foreground is the polished brass dome of the ship's binnacle housing the compass.*

Nearly half the vessels on this list were built in the first half of this century, and some have already exceeded their expected lifetime; but with modern technology and regular refits, some of the older vessels will serve for years to come. The USSR has some of the biggest square riggers still in commission, of which the *Sedov* is by far the largest. She carries a complement of 221 naval cadets and officers and is owned by the Ministry of Fisheries. She was originally designed as a cargo-cadet ship for FA Vinnen of Bremen, W Germany, and was built by the giant F Krupp at Kiel, Germany, in 1921. She is a four masted barque with a gross tonnage of 3,476 and an overall length of 329 ft (100 m). In 1936, she was sold by Vinnen's to the famous German shipping company Norddeutscher Lloyd. She came under Russian ownership at the end of World War II but following a refit, she was rarely outside Baltic waters until 1981. As four masters go, she was not dissimilar to the big barques of the Flying 'P' Line.

The *Mir* and the four masted barque *Kruzenshtern* also belong in the Russian fleet, along with the recently constructed *Druzhba*, built for the Superior Maritime School of Odessa. Of the three, the *Kruzenshtern* is the more interesting. Built of steel in 1926 as the *Padua*, she was one of the last great barques ordered by Carl Laeisz's Flying 'P' Line of Hamburg, founded by his father, Ferdinand B Laeisz, in 1824. He began his commercial career manufacturing silk hats in his home town of Bahia, Brazil, and purchased his first ship, a 22-year-old wooden schooner called *Sophie & Fredericke,* in 1856. That same year, Laeisz ordered a new ship, a 140 ft (42.6 m) barque called *Pudel* (poodle) apparently named in honour of his son Carl's wife Sophie who was endowed with thick, curly hair. Thereafter, all ships of the line had names beginning with the letter P.

The Flying 'P' Line went from strength to strength, increasing its tonnage by thousands as each decade passed. Ferdinand Laeisz had shrewdly recognized early on that Europe's

farmers, struggling to feed rapidly growing populations, desperately needed fertilizers. His contacts in South America were to prove useful. Nitrate became the company's staple cargo, shipped out from ports along the Chilean coast – Pisagua, Iquique, Tocopilla.

The 'P' liners became known as 'the nitrate clippers' because of their fast turn-around times and quick passages back to Europe. In truth, they were really just fast bulk carriers, so large and strong and carrying acres of canvas that only a handful of other shipping companies could compete effectively. Laeisz drove his ships hard, but not in an unseaman-like manner. His cap-

tains were given incentives to produce the best sailing times, outward bound and homeward. Where possible, a ship's standing and running gear was repaired rather than replaced at the end of each round voyage, the ship's sailmaker and carpenter being in constant employment.

Regular sailing schedules departing from German ports were organized, so that the 'P' liners could be expected to arrive at loading ports within a day, or two at the outside, of estimated times of arrival given to agents working for the line. Sometimes, when weather conditions on the 330 mile (528 km) leg around Cape Horn were at storm

force and blowing in the wrong direction, a ship could take five or six days, in some cases up to a fortnight, to round the bottom of South America. Laeisz's captains endeavoured to make swift passage around the Horn and were rarely held up for more than a day or two.

The agent's job was to organize lighterage (to take off the incoming cargo as the ship entered the roadstead anchorage). Other lighters already loaded with bags of guano would be standing by ready to come alongside the ship as hold space was made ready. Specialist stevedores, experienced in loading the cargo in pyramid formations would be assigned to each 'P' liner as soon as it anchored. With enough men to work in each hold, a big barque could be discharged and loaded in 10–14 days, ready to get under way and set course for home as the last bags were hoisted aboard. The off-watch crew, under the guidance of the bosun and ship's carpenter, would batten down hatches and secure the tarpaulins while those on the yards loosed top gallant sails as the mate ordered the last lighter cast off.

Laeisz liner captains wasted no time and set many records for the passage times to

BOTTOM LEFT: *Norway's 'Christian Radich' (left) and Poland's 'Dar Pomorza' prepare to set sail off Plymouth, England.*

Europe via the Horn. In 1895, the five masted barque *Potosi* was launched. She could stow a cargo of 6,000 tons (6,096 t) and was powered by 55,000 sq ft (16,764 sq m) of canvas. The average passage time from Europe to Chile was 75–80 days, but the *Potosi* set a new record of 66 days outward on her maiden voyage. In subsequent years, only the giant *Preussen* managed to reduce that, to a mere 57 days.

The *Padua (Kruzenshtern)* was no exception to the high average speeds attained by 'P' liners in the late 1800s and early 1900s: 11 or 12 knots was normal for these ships in a good breeze. Such was Carl Laeisz's optimism about the future of sail that in the same year as the *Padua* was launched, he ordered another four master, the *Priwall*.

He had already managed to buy back five older 'P' line ships that had been distributed as war reparations to a number of countries after World War I (1914–18). These included the *Peking*, the *Parma*, *Passat*, and the *Pamir*. The last was sadly lost at sea after foundering in an Atlantic hurricane southwest of the Azores in 1957. On her maiden voyage, the *Padua* transported nitrate from Talcahauno, and she remained on this run

TOP RIGHT:
The great four masted barque 'Kruzenshtern' under full sail off Plymouth and approaching the Isle of Wight. The ship is operated by the Russian Ministry of Fisheries.

RIGHT: *The world's largest square rig sailing ship, the Russian 'Sedov', sails out of the rain and mist off Plymouth, England on the first leg of the 1990 Tall Ships Race.*

ABOVE: *The Norwegian square riggers 'Christian Radich' and the 'Statsraad Lehmkuhl' sailing in company in the English Channel.*

for a few years, alternating occasionally with grain loaded on the Australian coast. But the nitrate trade was dying a slow death, and Laeisz laid up the *Padua* and the *Priwall*, sold the *Passat* to Finn Gustaf Erikson, and turned the *Peking* into a school training ship for company cadets. At the outbreak of war in 1939, she was transferred to the Baltic for safety reasons.

At the end of World War II, the Russians took the *Padua*, and after a lengthy refit, she was sent back to sea in the same role that Laeisz had had her converted for. Since then, she has sailed many thousands of miles and taken part in innumerable sail parades around the world.

The *Statsraad Lehmkuhl* was launched in 1914 from JC Tecklenborg's yard at Wismar on the Baltic coast for Deutscher Schulschiff Verein, specially built of steel as an auxiliary barque rigged sail training ship. She sailed first under the name of *Grosserherzog Friedrich August*, but in 1923 she was sold to Bergen Skolskib of Norway and renamed. She was seized by Germany during the Occupation of World War II, but she survived and was returned to her proprietors, Bergen Skolskib of Torvalmenning, and has been sailing successfully ever since.

Square rigged on the main and foremast, she carries a gaff mizzen carrying 6,500 sq ft (2,000 sq m) of sail handled by 24 officers and 180 cadet sailors. Her original auxiliary engine has been replaced with a powerful diesel engine to help with manoeuvering in confined waterways.

One of the prettiest three masted barques sailing as a training ship is the Portuguese Navy's *Sagres II*. She was built in 1937 by Blohm and Voss at Hamburg as the *Albert Leo Schlageter* and was used as a school ship for the German Navy. During the war, the vessel was employed as a stores transport around the Baltic Sea and was badly damaged by a floating mine. Recovered by the Americans, along with another square rigger, the *Horst Wessel* (now the *USCG Eagle*), she was handed over to the Brazilian Government who renamed her *Guanabara*. She was purchased by Portugal in 1962 to replace *Sagres I*.

Sagres II carries just under 6,500 sq ft (1,935 sq m) of sail and is crewed by 10 officers, 19 petty officers, 134 sailors and 80 cadets – quite a large complement for a relatively small ship! She is easily recognized by the huge, red Maltese crosses which adorn all of her square sails set on the main

took her as a war prize in 1916, renamed her *Flores*, and continued to use her for cargo carrying until 1924 when she was converted for use as a sail training ship, renamed yet again to become the first *Sagres*. She served in this capacity until 1962 when she was given yet another name – the *Santo Andre* – derigged and used as a depot ship in Portugal's Lisbon Harbour. In May 1983, she was towed to Hamburg where she has since been restored to her former glory as a museum ship.

The United States Coastguard barque *Eagle* was built and launched a year prior to the *Sagres II* by the same builders and given the name *Horst Wessel*. Built as another school ship for Hitler's navy, this 1,900 ton (1,930 t) barque was seized by the Americans as war reparations after the Allies took the port of Bremen. Now she is fitted with modern navigational equipment and a large auxiliary engine affectionately known as 'Elmer'. Her 22 sails get an airing once a year when she heads across the Atlantic to Europe or south from her home port of New London on America's eastern seaboard. She carries 19 officers, 26 petty officers and sailors, and 180 United States Coastguard cadets.

West Germany's *Gorch Fock*, a three masted barque, is operated by the Federal German Navy and carries 78 officers and sailors as well as 120 cadets. She was built in 1958 by Blohm and Voss of Hamburg to replace an earlier vessel of the same name built in 1932, which subsequently went on to become the Russian sail trainer *Tovarisch*. Apart from Argentina's *Libertad*, launched two years earlier, the *Gorch Fock* is the oldest of the post-war windjammers and has participated in nearly all of the great parades of sail since their inception in 1956. Her rig is fairly typical of that favoured by German sailing ship masters of pre-war years, setting royals and single t'gallants over double topsails. She also sports a double spanker set on the mizzen for ease of handling.

One odd ship out is the *Amerigo Vespucci*. An Italian vessel, launched in 1931, she was

and fore masts. Now more than 50 years old, she is seen infrequently in northern European waters.

Built in 1896 as the *Rickmer Rickmers* by and for the Rickmers firm at Bremerhaven, the *Sagres I* had had a colourful career. She sailed under a variety of flags and names while being employed on the Orient trade carrying coal out from Germany and returning with rice and bamboo, and then was transferred to the west coast of South America to carry nitrates. The Portuguese

designed by Commander Francesco Rotundi to resemble a ship of the line of the late 1700s. Whenever she takes part in the Cutty Sark races, or makes a courtesy visit to a foreign port during her annual three monthly cruise programme, there is little mistaking her. Both prow and stern are ornately decorated with a gilded figurehead, trailboards and stern carvings. She carries a number of small sailing and pulling gigs in davits, and when in port she can often be seen swarming with cadets in the process of keeping the ship gleaming and spotless.

Amerigo Vespucci was launched from the Italian Navy shipyard at Castellammare di Stabia in Naples. She is a three decked, three masted ship carrying 22,000 sq ft (6,705 sq m) of sail and fitted with a large auxiliary diesel engine. Her annual programme is extensive, comprising a 100 day course for the 160 or so first course cadets from the Naval Academy. Thirteen officers and 228 sailors provide additional manning of the ship. In the nearly 60 years she has been in commission, the ship has sailed many hundreds of thousands of miles visiting ports in North and South America, northern Europe and the Mediterranean, from her home base of La Spezia, Italy.

In addition to these great ships, many smaller vessels – mostly brigs, brigantines and schooners – take part in the sail parades and are also often engaged independently in earning a living. Film work, oceanographic

expeditions, tourist charters to exotic islands and the private training of youngsters is how most of them earn enough to pay the ever-mounting refit costs, running costs and harbour dues.

The vast majority of these old wooden hulled ships were formerly employed in the coasting trades of Great Britain and the Baltic. Many Baltic traders were still working cargo ships until as recently as the mid 1960s and early 1970s, some of them having worked almost a century since being launched. Others, such as the Finnish-built *Stina* and the Danish-built *Phoenix*, both of wood and rigged now as a schooner and brigantine, were not sent down the launchways until the 1930s and 1940s. The 72 ft (22 m) *Zebu* was another Baltic trader, taken out of retirement and refitted on Oulton Broad near Lowestoft, England. Rigged as a modern brigantine, she carries lightweight sails of duradon. In 1985, the *Xebu* sailed from Great Britain on a four year circumnavigation as part of Operation Raleigh, an expedition designed to take young people and students on an adventure they would never forget. The Swedish-built barquentine *Black Pearl* (ex *Eolus*), was launched in 1949 by her builders, Pukaviks Gamla Skepps; rigged as a 262 ton (266 t) auxiliary schooner, she traded Baltic ports out of Gothenburg until 1969 when she was sold into private hands.

Under the name of *Eolus*, the vessel came to England and a charter operation was set

1 Flying Jib
2 Outer Jib
3 Inner Jib
4 Fore Staysail
5 Fore Course
6 Fore Lower Topsail
7 Fore Upper Topsail
8 Fore Lower Topgallant
9 Fore Upper Topgallant
10 Fore Royal
11 Main Course
12 Main Lower Topsail
13 Main Upper Topsail
14 Main Lower Topgallant
15 Main Upper Topgallant
16 Main Royal
17 Crossjack
18 Mizzen Lower Topsail
19 Mizzen Upper Topsail
20 Mizzen Lower Topgallant
21 Mizzen Upper Topgallant
22 Mizzen Royal
23 Spanker
24 Main Staysail
25 Main Topmast Staysail
26 Main Topgallant Staysail
27 Mizzen Staysail
28 Mizzen Topmast Staysail

ABOVE: *'Maria Asumpta', with stunsails set, glides up the Solent on a balmy summer afternoon.*

LEFT: *The crew of the British square rigger 'Kaskelot' man the yards.*

DETAILS OF SAIL AND YARD

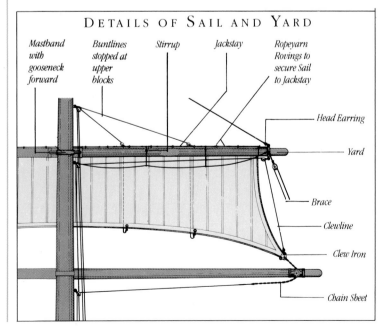

Mastband with gooseneck forward

Buntlines stopped at upper blocks

Stirrup

Jackstay

Ropeyarn Rovings to secure Sail to Jackstay

Head Earring

Yard

Brace

Clewline

Clew Iron

Chain Sheet

up to re-enact a voyage to Australia to celebrate the landing of the first voluntary migrants; the project came unstuck through
lack of finance. For a while the *Eolus* went
back to trading on the East African coast,
but by 1982 she had worked her way back
into the Mediterranean under her new name.
Misfortune seemed to haunt the ship; she
twice foundered and was salvaged in Maltese
waters. Her salvors eventually hauled the
ship ashore, poured concrete around her
hull and planned to use the vessel's remains
as a bar and restaurant.

So many of these Scandinavian wooden
vessels were built over the years that only
scant details are known of their where-
abouts; some, like the few mentioned above,
have been rebuilt, converted and restored,
and are sailing worldwide. But many, many
others have long since gone to Davy Jones

ABOVE: *One of the prettiest
of the smaller wooden
square riggers afloat, the
brigantine 'Zebu' arrives
in the Solent in 1984 prior
to taking part in Operation
Raleigh.*

RIGHT: *The brig 'Astrid'
built as a sailing schooner
and converted to a motor
coaster, was then gutted by
fire. She was saved from a
scrapyard and fully
restored to sail in 1989.*

Locker or been scrapped because the wooden shipowners' plague of rot, nail sickness and plain old age have rendered them unseaworthy.

Iron and steel hulled vessels have in a way proved more viable for shipowners, although steel has a tendency to erode quickly if not cared for. In recent years, one of the most remarkable restorations of an old steel sailing ship took place in England. The *Astrid*, built at Scheveningen in Holland in 1919 as the steel topsail schooner *Wuta*, sailed between Scandinavian ports and the Mediterranean for 35 years. In the 1970s she was employed on the Baltic trade routes as a motor coaster, her masts and sails having long since been left on the dockside.

Later in that decade, while registered under the Lebanese flag, British customs officers had reason to believe that she might be involved in the drug trade. When the duty men requested to board her while she was on passage in the English Channel, her crew took fright, poured fuel oil over the accommodation, and fired the ship. The hulk was towed to Newhaven, England, for scrap.

A young entrepreneur, David Barnett, on the lookout for a hull he could convert to a

square rigger, invested his life's savings in the gutted, rusting hulk and had it towed to the Hamble River on England's south coast. There she lay for another five years, her owner unable to raise the funds necessary for what was a major refit. The *Astrid* was sold on, this time to the one-time owner of Britain's greatest 'J' Class America's Cup racer, *Endeavour*. An ex-naval commander, Graham Neilson, also in search of a square rigger, struck a deal with her new owner John Amos and almost immediately set about founding the Astrid Trust so that her refit could take place.

In 1989, completely restored, rebuilt and rigged as a brig, the *Astrid* sailed into the Pool of London to take part in the Cutty Sark Tall Ships Parade of Sail. She is one of the prettiest sailing ships afloat and will be much admired wherever she sails.

Chapter Three

RIGS AND RIGGING

THE TERM 'RIG' DESCRIBES THE dis-tinctive arrangement of a vessel's masts, spars and sails. Since man discovered that the wind could propel a vessel through the water, the quest for greater speed and efficiency has encouraged the development of a whole variety of rigs as well as technological breakthroughs in hull design. The Egyptian Ship of c2500 BC sported a single square sail. The Greeks, Romans, Vikings and Normans all employed similar rigs on hulls peculiar to the various waters in which they sailed, and as design development continued at a painfully slow pace through the centuries, sailors worldwide borrowed the technology of the day from whatever caught their eye. The triangular lateen rigs of Spanish caravels of 1470 lent minor improvements to the dumpy English carrack of 1485, itself possibly copied from a similar rig built by the Flemish a few years earlier.

LEFT: *A maze of rigging on the 'Libertad'. Her sails are raised and lowered from the deck using halyards running through blocks on the yards secured to the foot of each sail.*

Gradually ships grew in size. More masts carried more sail: an enormous square sail would have been impractical, so it was cut into smaller areas and rigged one on top of the other. Sailors discovered that by adding triangular sails to the foremast and rigging them to a large spar projecting forward over the prow of the ship, which was fixed there to help support the forward mast, forces acting on the aftermost sails were counteracted in certain conditions, making the vessel easier to control in winds that came from forward of the beam.

The basic rig of the Elizabethan galleon of 1600 spawned many merchant and warships using variations of the design. As hull design over the ensuing decades was slowly refined, so too was the rig. This culminated in the three masted full rigged ships of the East Indiamen of 1815 and onward, with their long, slender hulls supporting three masts, on which were rigged 14 or more square sails of varying size, three staysails of triangular cut, rigged between the aftermost, main and foremast, four headsails, and a spanker (or jigger), rigged on the aftermost, or mizzen mast. Half a century later hulls were even more refined, the masts carried more sails, and greater speeds thus became possible.

The square rigged ship, and the barque which was to follow, became the most functional and arguably one of the most efficient of man's creations. The rig was developed to take advantage of the constant wind patterns of the world, enabling a sailing vessel to voyage to nearly all parts of the globe with the wind coming from abaft the beam. Experienced and knowledgeable sailing ship masters invariably managed to achieve high average speeds and great noon to noon runs on both outward and homeward passages. Anything less than 300 miles a day – noon to noon – was considered poor performance, especially by owners of the larger barques engaged on scheduled routes.

But while the trade winds could be relied upon for the most part, the sailing ship usually had cause to seek towage assistance

The ultimate development of the square rig produced ships with large numbers of smaller sails, fitted in such a manner that they could easily be 'clewed up' (a term taken from clew irons) by smaller crews. Masts and standing rigging were designed to withstand the huge stresses put upon them by masters anxious to reap the extra bounty for a fast passage. Shipowners, while recognizing that smaller crews meant less overheads for them, were also careful to acknowledge the safety factor in keeping sailors alive while working aloft. A well managed ship worked efficiently; it could not be as efficient if already small crews were more diminished by unnecessary accidents caused by poor rigging aloft. Each part of the rig, from clew irons to brace winches, was developed from the practical experience of working a ship on long ocean voyages.

The weather conditions under which men were sometimes required to work aloft were often appalling, but individual voyages were more often than not straightforward, sailed in fair weather from port to port and requiring little work on the upper yards and even less on the lower ones. On a fair weather passage, the only trimming of sails that might be required from time to time could easily be accomplished from the deck by working the brace winches and trimming sheets. The royals, upper topsails and topgallants might occasionally require their yards to be tweaked a little, so they were pitched slightly finer to the apparent wind than the main course and crossjack sails set below. The various angles of the yards set in relation to the main course yard are an indicator of how well the ship is being sailed. The velocity and angle of wind attack will differ slightly at sea level from the angle and velocity 180–200 ft (55–60 m) higher at the mast truck, which is why in many old pictures of square riggers depicted blasting through the ocean in the trades, the sails appear to be set in a somewhat corkscrew fashion.

The head, or top, of each sail is attached to the yard. To furl it onto the yard requires the two clew lines, or sheets, one at each

when making a landfall. Once in sight of land, winds would drop, or the ship would be caught by an offshore breeze forcing her to drop anchor and wait for hours, sometimes days, until conditions changed.

An exception to this was off the west coast of Australia, where a very predictable onshore breeze could be relied upon to take ships waiting in Gage Roads off Fremantle harbour, up the Swan River to Perth. The 'Fremantle Docker', as it was originally called in the 1890s, could be spotted by observant watchkeepers on anchored ships as it swept in from the Indian Ocean, first as a ripple on a glassy sea, and later blowing white caps off the waves at a steady 20 knots. Whatever its strength, few masters had cause to call out the tug until they were well inside the harbour breakwater, preparing to reduce sail.

bottom corner of the sail, to be let go from the deck. As this is done, the men manning the yard gather up and literally beat the wind out of the sail by smashing their fists against the canvas and pulling the sail down onto the yard. Hard enough when the sails were dry, but when they were sodden, the work was painfully slow; added to freezing temperatures, freezing spray and hypothermia, the work took its toll on the men.

To secure the sail in place, gaskets or ties are placed around the canvas and the whole is lashed to the yard. To set the sail, the gaskets are removed first, light lines, or bunt-lines (sometimes also called clewlines) are attached and are all that now hold the sail to the yard. A good yank on the sheets by the crew on deck is enough to part the line so the sail can be set.

Staysails, the triangular-shaped sails set between the masts, are set by having a halyard attached to their head, and sheets on the clew. The sail is hoisted on the halyard and set with the sheets.

When a ship changes its heading from one tack to another, the angle of the yards

THE UBIQUITOUS BLOCK

IN A SAILING SHIP, the pulley wheel, or block as it is more commonly known, is an essential item of equipment in the vessel's inventory of running rigging. Used as a single pulley to halve the mechanical load, the block performs innumerable duties from use in a simple davit (crane), trimming the sheets of a sail, hoisting a sail and as a lead through which halyards and sheets are run, to the more complicated two, three and four block arrangements which are set up aboard ship, allowing one man to do the work of many. The special names allocated to certain blocks denote a special function. The following are just a few of the many different types to be found on board a square rigged ship.

Bull's eye, butterfly, cat block, dead-eye, double block, fiddle, hook block, jack, leading block, monkey block, ninepin, purchase blocks, running block, secret, sister block, swivel, tack, top block and waist block.

supporting the square sails also has to be changed. The crew working on deck use the bracing winches to wind the great steel yards around to the best angle of attack on the wind. All the yards are controlled in this fashion, although today many modern windjammers have electric or hydraulically-operated winches to assist the process. In the days of the great grain races or the nitrate trade, winches were mostly hand-operated; only in very rare cases were they steam-assisted. The replacement of the wire rope purchase found on earlier vessels with a handraulic winch was a luxury for most seamen.

Tacking a barque through the eye of the wind was a complicated manoeuver which sailing ship masters would have preferred to avoid, especially when they were closing a dangerous coast or a lee shore. A big ship needs a good hull speed and plenty of sea room for these manoeuvers before the helm can be put down. If it was put down too quickly, the ship would simply lose her way and have to pay off on the same tack before more speed could be gathered and another attempt made.

The procedure went as follows; shortly before the tacking, the master would order 'ready about!'; the sheets were eased so the ship could pay off the wind a little and gather more speed. As the order 'tack ship' was given, the helm went down to weather; under the tremendous momentum built up as the ship had eased off the wind, she would slowly come up head to wind. The spanker on the mizzen was hauled forcefully across to weather to help push the stern around, keeping the momentum going and maintaining steerage way. Flaying canvas, blocks banging against the masts and yards, and orders being shouted from the bridge deck to the sail trimmers create a tremendous noise.

The sails are aback, helping to push the bow of the ship across the wind. The main course yard is hauled around, so the sail will quickly fill and keep the vessel moving ahead. The foresails, or jibs are sheeted in

tight. With sails on the foremast now aback, the vessel pays off rapidly to leeward; the yards and sheets are trimmed as the ship gathers way on her new tack.

Much of the work of sailing a windjammer is done from the deck, particularly with modern vessels. Technology from ocean racing yachts has been developed to help with the management of lighter terylene sails, which are commonly used in place of the old cotton canvas. Although fatal accidents involving men in the yards did happen, they were infrequent, and mostly the result of poor maintenance aloft or of fatigue and cold during a storm.

The 'standing' part of the rigging is literally that: the fixed wires and ropes which hold up the masts. It was relatively easy to devize ways of utilizing the standing parts to form ladders – called ratlines – which provided safe and easy access to the sails and yards aloft. Hemp rope was tied across and then whipped with light cod line on standing parts to form the rungs. After a little practice, those working aloft could climb with ease in fair weather, although in bad weather it was a different story. It could take ages for even the most experienced

THE SPLICE

A METHOD OF JOINING lengths of rope or wire rope, or one of each to the other, for the making of eyes in a length of rope. The parts to be joined are first unlayed until the several strands of each part are separated. Depending on the size of the rope or wire, instruments called fids and marline spikes are used to part the strands of the standing part of each rope so that the separated strand of the tail can be passed through in a series of 'tucks'. When the required number of tucks is completed the rope or wire is 'served' and 'whipped' to prevent loose ends of the splice from fraying or, in a wire, from snagging.

FAR LEFT: *These steel masts with steel yards fixed on swivels set with lightweight terylene sails are controlled from the deck on a modern square rigger.*

RIGHT: *Boomed staysails on the three masted schooner 'Aquarius' at sea off Western Australia.*

LEFT: *Wire brace and halyard winches of the type introduced on the big windjammers plying the South American nitrate trade. These helped shipowners cut crew costs, and are seen here on the 'Pommern'.*

sailors to climb aloft. The only safe way to do this was to take the ratlines (pronounced ratlins) on the weather side. When the ship pitched or rolled violently, the force of the wind would be more than enough to keep a man firmly pressed against the shrouds so that he would literally have to fight a way to the yard where trouble was brewing. Once on the yard, footropes rigged on the lower part of the yard, handlines and the yard itself were all a man had to hang onto. Frequently, because he needed both hands to work with, only the weight of his body pressed against the yard and his feet kept him from falling. But fall they did, and there are some great yarns spun by old salts about how far they fell before a flaying rope or a billowing canvas caught them up short!

LEFT: *The barquentine training ship 'Leeuwin' sports two modern yacht-type spinnakers in her forerig; they appear to be pulling well.*

At the turn of the century, an alternative to the big, square rigged ship became apparent. The high aspect fore and aft rig used on sailing yachts and smaller coasting vessels required few hands to manage it, and the speeds attained by some of these smaller vessels were impressive. In the desperate fight against the age of cheap fuel and steam power, shipowners and designers developed the fore and aft schooner rig, taken from the fast topsail schooner slave ships and Baltimore clippers of the 1830s. While it was very efficient on smaller vessels, it proved hopelessly impractical on the larger ships which eventually came to wear it, as seen below.

	PENAG (barque)	AMERICAN SCHOONER (built 1907)
Length	268 ft (81.5 m)	270 ft (82 m)
Mast height	140 ft (42.5 m)	190 ft (58 m)
Number of masts	3	6
Sail area	26,000 sq ft (7,925 sq m)	20,000 sq ft (6,096 sq m)
Largest sail	2,880 sq ft (878 sq m)	6,000 sq ft (1,829 sq m)

The area of a single, big ship schooner sail was immense, more than three times the size of the whole sail area of an ocean-going 40 ft (12 m) yacht. Even with their

ABOVE: *Neatly stowed sheets hang on the shroud pin rail across which ratlines of the brigantine 'Barba Negra' form a picture window on the sailing ship 'Wavertree'.*

RIGHT: *The 800 ton (813 t) 'Creoula', one of the few remaining four masted fore and aft rigged schooners. A veteran of 37 fishing voyages to the Grand Banks, she now trains youngsters under the Portuguese flag.*

comparatively sophisticated array of steam-driven winches, these giant sails often caused problems for undermanned crews.

In 1902, the 5,218 ton (5,301 t) steel-built American schooner *Thomas W Lawson* was launched with seven masts, rigged fore and aft on each one. She had an overall length of 395 ft (120 m) and was the largest commercial schooner ever built. Her 135 ft (41 m) steel masts were topped with 58 ft (17.5 m) of pine to give some flexibility to the rig in a bad seaway. Her seven masts were named fore, main, mizzen, jigger, spanker, driver and pusher. She was a commercial disaster in spite of being crewed by a mere 16 hands, capsizing five years after her launch off the Scilly Isles with the loss of all but one of her crew. A number of other similarly rigged vessels also foundered in bad weather.

When hit by a sudden squall, a schooner the size of the *Thomas W Lawson* increases the speed of the apparent wind by adding her own speed through the water to the squall. Under these conditions, the power of the wind could, at times, be close to that of a full hurricane, putting the stability of the ship on the margin. A square rigged ship would pay off the wind by running away from a squall, reducing both its velocity and power on the sails, and consequently its risk of foundering, whereas vessels with a schooner rig headed into the wind so as to spill the wind out of the sails, thus increasing instability.

The large schooner was also compromized when sailing before the wind, while square riggers excelled at it. The schooner risked serious gybing, and eventual broaching leading to capsize, if the sailing master and his crew were not on their toes. A gybe occurs when the boom at the foot of the fore and aft mainsail is purposely swung from one side of the ship to the other. It can also happen if the wind suddenly changes direction, or if for some reason the helm is put up. So while theoretically possible, in practice the huge six or seven masted schooner was unwieldy, lacking the grace and elegance of a square rigged vessel.

ABOVE: *Cadets climb the ratlines of the Polish 'Dar Mlodzeizy'. All are wearing safety harnesses.*

In today's fleets, there are a number of smaller topsail, staysail and gaff schooners perfectly suited to the rig because of their relatively short overall length, modern winches, and plentiful crew. The British *Sir Winston Churchill* and the *Malcolm Miller* are two examples of relatively recent construction designed for ease of handling in a variety of weather conditions.

Little has changed regarding the concept of these smaller rigged vessels over the last century. The ancestors of sail training ships, such as Holland's *Eendracht*, the Swedish *Gladan* or the French sister ships *Belle*

Poule and *Etoile*, were the Gloucester Grand Banks schooners which raced from their home ports on the East Coast of New England, US, to fishing grounds off Newfoundland in the early decades of this century.

These vessels measured between 120–130 ft (36–40 m) overall. Many were designed by BB Crowninshield and his junior, John Alden, who went on to become one of America's most respected yacht designers. In his early independent years, Alden used what he had learned from commercial sailing vessels in a range of smaller schooner rigged yachts he designed for private owners. Probably the fastest and most famous of all the Grand Banks schooners was *Bluenose*, designed by WJ Roue and built in the 1920s. In spite of their colossal sail areas, these ships could be handed by two or three men, necessary at times when the fishermen were out in the fishing grounds in the small dorys they carried on deck. Their speeds were impressive with a good wind, just as those of their modern counterparts are.

It is interesting to note that after so many years, large square rigged sailing vessels of a comparative size to the earlier wind-jammers continue to be built and launched. Methods of hull construction, design, and the design of masts and spars have developed with the times, but the essential ingredients of the rig as perfected in the latter half of the last century have largely remained untouched.

ABOVE: *The three masted schooner 'Bel Espoir', typical of the smaller, wooden hulled schooners which once plied the coasts of Europe and the Baltic.*

LEFT: *Officers of the watch on the Mexican 'Cuauhtemoc' study the set of sails, while a sailor prepares to break out signal flags.*

RIGHT: *Sailors man the yards to loose sail on the Venezuelan training ship 'Simon Bolivar'.*

Chapter Four

MUSEUM SHIPS OF THE WORLD

DOTTED AROUND THE WORLD, IN ports as far apart as Honolulu and Mariehamn, are the few remaining examples of an era which once counted their number in thousands. The age of steam and the worldwide shipping slump which followed World War I (1914–18) gradually made inroads into the great fleets of sailing ships. Rusting hulks were turned into floating pontoons, tied up in harbours row upon row and gradually fed back into white hot furnaces to be melted down and rolled out as new products. Just as many were lost in the natural course of seafaring, by running aground, foundering in horrific storms, being dashed on rocks or sucked into the moving sand and shingle of shallow beaches.

LEFT: *The Chilean navy's training barquentine 'Esmeralda' pictured in the Western Approaches.*

*R*ecords over the last few hundred years show that some 4,000 ships have been wrecked at the back of the Isle of Wight off the English coast, on a treacherous stretch of coast which runs from the Needles on the western end to Bembridge Ledge in the east. Of this number, a great many were sailing ships which drifted ashore in fog, sailed up the beach through navigational error, were stranded on rocks while trying to cut corners, dragged their anchors, or were in collision with other vessels.

The list of casualties reads like a telephone directory: the full rigged 900 ton (914 t) *Underley*, bound for Melbourne in 1871 with 30 migrants and a cargo of cotton goods, ended up on the rocks off Bonchurch when a spirited south easterly pushed her ashore; the iron built barque *Alpheta* ran onto Bembridge Ledge in 1877 and became a total loss; the 1,588 ton (1,613 t) *Sirenia* fetched ashore on Atherfield Ledge in a storm in 1888; the *Irex* became a total wreck off the Needles in January 1890, some of her timbers eventually being salvaged and used for the construction of cottages in the nearby village of Freshwater; the full rigged ship *Alcester*, out of Liverpool and sailing from Calcutta to Hamburg, was lost on Atherfield Ledge in 1897 – she broke in two and became a total

wreck; in the same place, the German barque *Auguste* met her end in February 1900; the *Carl*, a full rigged ship, was driven into Freshwater Bay by high tides and gale force winds, her crew scrambling to safety over the bowsprit. Her fate was more fortunate, however; she sailed again after a channel had been blasted through the shingle and the vessel hove off by tugs.

Wreckings and strandings such as these were commonplace wherever tall ships sailed on the trade routes of the world. Their safest haven was the deep ocean. Land was a menace; a sailing ship master needed all his skill to keep his ship from driving ashore in inclement weather, although occasionally it was not only weather which was the menace. When the Glasgow-built full rigged ship *Glenesslin* fetched up on the rocks beneath Neahkahnie Mountain on the Oregon coast of North America, she did so in style. She was 176 days out from Santos, Brazil in ballast for the Columbia River when on 1 October, 1913, a clear and fine day, the ship drove ashore with all sail set. At the hearing which followed, the blame for the wrecking was laid to incompetence, a patch of calm inside a nearby headland, and drink.

Ships which have survived to this day, and which have been lovingly restored for the

LEFT: *While on a voyage from Sweden to Melbourne with timber and pig-iron, the 'Hansey' was wrecked in Housel Bay near Lizard Point, Cornwall, in November 1911. She was trying to tack ship in a gale.*

ARETHUSA TRAINING SHIP.   H.7787.

public to see, are the lucky few. These were either converted to steam by shipowners when it became obvious that steam would take over the world's merchant ship fleets, or ended their working lives being used as bulk storage hulks, or, as in the case of the *Peking*, passed into more benevolent hands and were put to good use as static training ships. Others, discovered lying to rot on a distant shore, have been brought back to life by dint of volunteer enthusiasm, but these are now few and far between.

GUSTAF ERIKSON, THE PAMIR, PASSAT and POMMERN
In the years immediately following World War I, when many ships were changing hands at scrap prices, or being given away as war reparations, one man had the foresight – some called it foolhardiness – to begin buying a number of tall ships. Gustaf Erikson was a native of the island of Aland which lay some 25 miles off the Swedish coast and which had been ceded to Finland by the League of Nations but retained autonomy.

Mariehamn, Finland's second port, was Erikson's headquarters, although he saw little of it in his early sailing life. When he retired from deep sea voyaging at the age of 41, he bought the Scottish-built *Renee Rickmers* and renamed her *Aland*; she struck a reef and was lost on her first voyage out under

Erikson's ownership. Undeterred, he bought more ships, including the *Grace Harwar*, the four masted *Lawhill*, the *Olivebank* and a number of others. His greatest affection was for the four masted barque *Herzogin Cecile*, built originally for the German Norddeutscher-Lloyd line. In April 1936, she was bound up the English Channel for Ipswich, on England's east coast. The captain, Sven Eriksson, was accompanied by his young bride and was using the voyage partly as a honeymoon trip.

A moderate sea was running with a light south westerly breeze when a sea mist closed in around the ship. Unknown to Eriksson at the time, he was off course, too far to the north of his track. Suddenly, the huge barque was hard aground among rocks off Bolt Head on the Devon coast. Everyone aboard managed to get ashore unscathed, but this magnificent ship became a total loss in the ensuing weeks as tugs attempted to tow her off. Badly holed, her cargo of grain wet through, she was eventually scrapped. Her loss badly affected Gustaf Erikson, who at the peak of his ownership career had amassed some 20 windjammers and managed to keep them all in trade.

From 1925–1935, Erikson had purchased seven steel four masted barques. Among these were the *Pamir*, the *Moshulu* and the

ABOVE: 'Asgard II',
Ireland's wooden-hulled
sail training ship, behind a
huge wave in the Western
Approaches as she heads out
towards the Bay of Biscay
in company with a British
schooner.

Passat. With the coming of World War II, Erikson gradually began to lay up or disperse the ships to safer havens. The *Pamir*, originally a Laeisz line nitrate clipper, sailed under the British flag for part of the war but on arrival at Wellington in 1941 she was seized by the New Zealand government. Two years later she began trading again, this time across the Pacific to the United States. In December 1947 she arrived in London to a blaze of publicity, 80 days out from Wellington with a cargo of tallow and wool, There was talk of a revival of the great days of sail.

Sadly, Erikson was not to witness the return of this famous ship for in August that same year he died, aged 75. The New Zealand government returned the ship to Erikson's son and the *Pamir* made another voyage to Australia for grain in 1948. The following year, both she and the *Passat* made the last commercial grain runs from Australia under sail.

By all accounts Erikson's son Edgar was not that interested in sail and two years later, the two ships were towed to Antwerp for scrapping. A German shipowner, Heinz Schliewen, bought both ships and had them converted to cargo-cadet ships. Both vessels were given auxiliary engines, fitted out with the latest navigational equipment, and placed back in the South American trade carrying about 60 cadets. Schliewen went bankrupt and again the ships changed hands, being purchased by a German consortium who were sail training enthusiasts.

In 1957, *Pamir* loaded grain in Buenos Aires. Instead of it being loaded in bags, as was the common practice on the Australian route, this South American cargo was loaded in bulk and packed down with a few bags across the top of the cargo. Bulk cargoes of this nature were fine in a steamer, which stayed upright for most of its voyaging, but in a square rigger which sailed with a permanent list to one side because of the pressure of wind on her sails, it was extremely bad stowage practice.

On the home run while about 400 miles (640 km) west south west of the Azores, Hurricane Carrie struck the *Pamir*. Her cargo shifted, and distress calls were sent by radio. Several ships went to her assistance, but it was too late. In spite of managing to get most of her sail off, the crew were not able to save her. She rolled over and sank with the loss of 80 lives.

Only two weeks after this disaster had struck, the *Passat*, loaded with a cargo of barley stowed in the same fashion, ran into a severe gale and began to list heavily to port. Her captain, who had heard about the fate of the *Pamir*, had the presence of mind to fill his already grain-filled starboard ballast tanks with water. The ship was saved and he was able to make port at Lisbon where the cargo was restowed. Such was the public outcry following the loss of the *Pamir* that the owners of the *Passat* reluctantly decided to end her days as a commercial voyager. Now she is a static museum ship at Travemunde, West Germany.

At Mariehamn, the last remaining ship of Gustaf Erikson's grain fleet remains as a tribute to the man whose faith in sail never faltered. The floating museum was made possible through the generosity of Gustaf's son, Edgar, and daughter, Eva Hohenthal.

The *Pommern* was built at Reid's yard on the banks of the River Clyde in Scotland and was launched in 1903 as the *Mneme* for the shipping company Wenck of Hamburg. She has a gross tonnage of 2,456 (2,495 t), is 311 ft (95 m) long and is rigged as a four masted barque. She was a fast ship in her time and it was this which persuaded the inimitable Laeisz firm to make a bid for her in 1907. Renamed, she twice ran from the Lizard, Cornwall, to Valpariso, Chile, in 65 days. After being interned on the South American west coast throughout World War I, she was taken as reparation by the Allies and handed to the Greek government in 1920. She was little used under the Greek flag and eventually voyaged to Delfzijl in Holland where she was offered for sale by tender.

Gustaf Erikson paid £3,750 ($7,500) for the hull and another £150 ($300) for the ship's stores. She was dry-docked in Emden, refitted, and sailed to Chile for a cargo of saltpetre. She remained on that run for approximately six years before she was transferred to the Australian grain run in 1929. She continued to sail the route right up until the outbreak of war. She made several good passages of between 94 and 129 days over the years but was finally laid up at Mariehamn, never to sail again. In 1953, Erikson's heirs gave the ship to the town where she now forms the major part of the Aland Maritime Museum. It contains a huge number of nautical exhibits including one of the finest collections of ships' figureheads and other ephemera culled from the Erikson, Algot Johansson and Lundqvist fleets which operated from the island.

FALLS OF CLYDE

Across the other side of the world, at the Bishop Museum in Honolulu, the full rigged, four masted ship *Falls of Clyde* lies majestically restored to her former glory. She was built by Russell & Co of Port Glasgow for world tramping, and was the first of nine vessels for the famous Falls line of Glasgow. All the ships were named after famous Scottish waterfalls: the *Falls of Garry*, the *Falls of Halladale*, the *Falls of Bruar*, the *Falls of Foyers* and the *Falls of Earn* all met undignified ends by wrecking. The *Falls of Dee* passed into Norwegian ownership and was sunk in 1917 by a German submarine. From her launch in 1878 until 1899, the *Clyde* travelled the world carrying a variety of general and bulk cargo.

In 1898, she was purchased by William Matson while berthed in San Francisco, and became one of the original Matson line ships. She arrived in Honolulu on 20 January, 1899 and was converted from a ship to a barque with a deck house and a charthouse added. Matson put her into regular service carrying sugar between Hilo and San Francisco – and re-registered her under the American flag the following year.

BELOW: *Another view of the barque 'Pommern' which clearly shows the huge size of her steel masts and yards.*

ABOVE: *The 'Falls of Clyde', pictured at her moorings at the Bishop Museum in Honolulu, Hawaii where she has been fully restored as a static museum.*

In 1907 she was sold to the Associated Oil Company and became something of a rarity when she was converted to a sailing oil tanker, making several charter voyages to Denmark, South America and Panama. In 1922, her yards and masts were sent down and she was towed to Alaska where she became a floating oil depot at Ketchikan under the ownership of the General Petroleum Company. In 1958 she was sold into private hands who had her towed to Seattle, where she might have become a log breakwater at Vancouver had it not been for the enthusiasm of the people of Hawaii and Captain F Klebingat, a former second mate of the ship who visited her in Seattle and found her in remarkably good condition. In 1963, enough money was raised by public subscription to purchase the hulk and have it towed to Honolulu where, under the ownership of the Bernice P Bishop Museum, founded in 1968, her complete restoration has taken place. She was constructed of riveted wrought iron with 11/16″ (1.7 cm) plates,

measured 266 ft (81 m) overall and had a gross tonnage of 1,807 (1,836 t). The generosity of the Hawaiian people apart, it was probably her wrought iron plates that saved the Clyde from an earlier demise, having withstood over 80 years of service.

STAR OF INDIA

Launched from the yard of Gibson, McDonald & Arnold at Ramsey, Isle of Man, as the full rigged ship *Euterpe* on 14 November, 1863, the *Star of India*, as she has long since been called, lays claim to being the oldest merchant ship still afloat. She lies in San Diego, California, her iron hull and rig so well restored that she has been able to put to sea once or twice in recent years.

Her home port was originally Liverpool, from where her Isle of Man owners had intended that she would run cargo and a small quota of passengers to India. She had been built with spacious 'tween decks and fitted with port holes along this strake, which would, inferred the publicity surrounding her launch, have made her eminently suitable as a troopship should the need have arisen.

Only a few hours after setting sail from Liverpool on her maiden voyage, she was in collision with a Spanish brig, which did extensive damage to her forerigging. The crew were so apprehensive of her seaworthiness, they demanded a return to port for repairs or they would refuse to sail the ship. Some of the crew were jailed for this impudence and missed her subsequent safe passage to Calcutta. Two years later, at the end of December 1864, the *Euterpe* sailed from Liverpool, again bound for ports in India and Sri Lanka (then Ceylon).

She did not return home for another 23 months, when in a hurricane off Madras on 29 November, 1866, she lost all three masts, took refuge in the harbour at Trincomalee and eventually sailed into Calcutta where she was rerigged. On the passage home, a few days out from India, her captain died of fever, leaving the mate to take command.

She changed ownership twice after this and spent time in the Indian coastal trade before being acquired by Shaw, Savill & Albion who specialized in long voyages from Great Britain to the Antipodes. *Euterpe* spent a number of years voyaging between London or Glasgow and Auckland or Wellington in New Zealand, mostly with cabin or emigrant passengers. She made more than a score of these long trips, sailing outward via the Cape of Good Hope, through the 'Roaring Forties', and homeward via Cape Horn to the English Channel.

The opening of the Suez Canal put an end to her usefulness under the Shaw Savill flag and she was subsequently sold to the Pacific Colonial Ship Company of San Francisco. She was placed under Hawaiian registry which enabled her, when that country became part of the United States, to obtain American registry. Her new owners filled her with timber, loaded in Puget Sound, and sent her packing to Australia where Douglas fir and Oregon pine were much in demand. On the voyage home, she would carry coal, to Honolulu where she then loaded a cargo of sugar for the last leg to the West Coast of America.

LEFT: *The world's largest square rig sailing ship, the Russian 'Sedov', sails out of the rain and mist off Plymouth, England on the first leg of the 1990 Tall Ships Race.*

Pacific Colonial sold the ship to the Alaska Packers Association of San Francisco, who were already the owners of several beautiful vessels acquired from the line affectionately known as 'Corry's Irish Stars'. These Harland & Wolff-built ships were some of the finest ever launched between 1877–1880, the *Star of Bengal* and the *Star of France* being noted worldwide for their speed. *Euterpe* was renamed *Star of India*, but her globe trotting days were numbered. The Packers sent her up to Alaska in the spring and back to the warmer climate of 'Frisco in autumn. Her rig was reduced too; instead of the five yards which once sprouted on her mizzen, now there was a huge spanker and topsail. As a barque, she was easier to handle with a smaller crew. New accommodations were built on the maindeck from the poop to the mainmast, large enough to carry at least 45 fishermen. The bright hardwood trim around her upperworks disappeared under layers of 'box-car red' paint and the once white bulwarks and deckhouses were painted a miserable buff colour. She made her last voyage to Alaska in 1923.

Had it not been for one James Wood Coffroth, *Star of India* might have ended her days as another breakwater in some obscure harbour. He bought the ship and gave her to the San Diego Zoological Society in 1926 with the idea that she should be fitted out as a floating museum and aquarium. But in the grim days of the American Depression, there was little spare cash available for such projects. Neglected, the great ship began to deteriorate. Paint cracked and peeled, decks leaked and the rigging was in a poor state of repair, quickly rotting under the unrelenting sun. During World War II, the US Navy declared her masts a hazard to aerial navigation and sent a party along to send down her yards and remove the topmasts. Tired of their gift, the Zoological Society gave the ship to the newly formed Maritime Museum Association in 1957.

The task of restoring her was colossal. Congress voted $17,000 (£8,500) towards her restoration in payment for the damage done

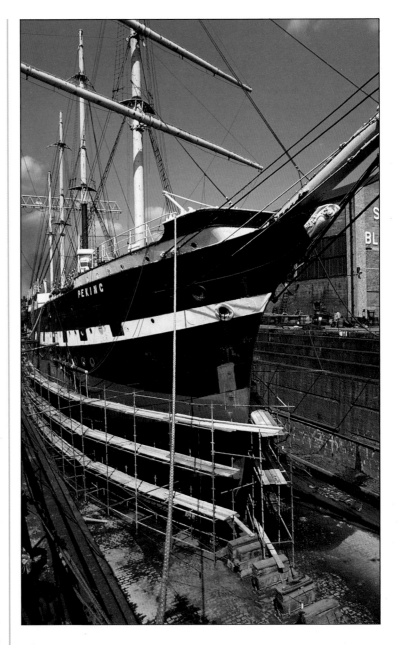

during the war. In 1963 she reached 100 and is now well into her second century. She is maintained exclusively by admission fees, donations and membership of the Museum Association. Her restoration was a painfully slow process because of the lack of skilled craftsmen and traditional materials, such as hemp, Stockholm tar and the many chandlery fittings needed to make her seaworthy. But she did sail again, 113 years after her launching and 53 years after her last voyage to Unimak Pass. Canvas billowing from her yards, she sailed out of San Diego and into the Pacific Ocean on Independence Day, 1976.

ABOVE: *The 'Peking' in dry dock on the River Thames, London, undergoing waterline replating before her last voyage across the Atlantic in 1975.*

PEKING

The *Peking* was another of the many vessels owned by Reederei F Laeisz GmbH. She was a four masted barque, built in Hamburg by Blohm and Voss in 1911 especially for the nitrate trade from South America. She could set 44,132 sq ft (13,451 sq m) of canvas and regularly, along with her sister ships, set passages of less than 70 days from the English Channel to Valpariso. She was interred in Valpariso until 1921 when she was handed over to Italy as war reparations. In 1923, Carl Laeisz managed to buy her back for the sum of £8,500 ($17,000) and three years later she was converted to a cargo-carrying school ship.

By 1932, some of the Laeisz ships went to Gustaf Erikson. The *Peking* was sold to the Shaftesbury Homes as a training ship and named *Arethusa II*, replacing an earlier vessel of the same name which had been built in 1849. After a £40,000 ($80,000) refit and conversion, the new *Arethusa* was moored on the Lower Upnor on the River Medway where she remained for the next 43 years.

Her top gallant masts were cut down until only a few feet remained at the doublings and all but two of her great yards were sent down. Her holds were fitted out with dormitories for 200–300 boys aged 13–15 who were given a thorough grounding in seamanship; many joined the Royal Navy when they left the *Arethusa*.

By 1974, the cost of maintaining this huge vessel was becoming enormous. Her plates at the waterline had become so thin that the vessel was a danger to herself, the people who trained on her, and navigation on the river. She was put up for sale.

Representative of a particular era in German seafaring, she was of little interest to British marine historians. The South Street Seaport Museum in New York, who were already in the process of restoring the *Wavertree* and who had previously towed the *Moshulu* across the Atlantic from Amsterdam, showed great interest in acquiring the *Arethusa*. (The *Moshulu*, by the way, featured in the opening sequences of the film *The Godfather II*).

BELOW: *Shipwrights and boilermakers carefully insert new steel plates along the waterline strake of the hull of the old 'Peking'.*

South Street dithered, however, and it became apparent that only a shipbreaker was interested in taking the hulk to the knackers yard. A preservation appeal was set up, backed by a Lloyds syndicate of 12 who guaranteed to make up any shortfall. The Arethusa Training Ship Society was on the point of going public with the appeal when back came South Street Seaport Musem. At an auction at Savill's of London, the ship was sold to the New York museum for £70,000 ($112,000).

Before she could be taken across .the Atlantic on her own bottom, considerable repairs to her shell plating was necessary. A dry docking and survey operation was put in hand by Commander H 'Hap' Paulsen, USCG Rtd, one-time skipper of America's own training ship, *USCG Eagle*. Given back her original name, the *Peking* was docked at RH Green's yard at Blackwall on the River Thames, London. Structural work began on

ABOVE: *The restored German barque 'Peking' in her berth on pier 16 at South Street Seaport Museum, New York.*

TOP LEFT: *The 'Gefion' (left) and the 'Lindo' from the United States and the Cayman Islands, measure 189 tons (192 t) and 176 tons (179 t) respectively and share similar hull shapes.*

BOTTOM LEFT: *The 'Peking' is towed across the Atlantic to her new home in New York.*

removing the rusted plates along her water-line. The ribs behind were found to be in good condition, so new strakes were welded in place at enormous cost: nearly £100,000 ($160,000) was spent on making her ready for sea. While this work was under way, Hap Paulsen searched for a tow. The Dutch sal-vage and towage firm of Wijsmuller BV came up with an ocean-going tug that was already on its way across the Atlantic for a two-year spell of stand-by duty based on Antigua.

When work on the *Peking* was complete, she was refloated in June 1975 and taken down the Thames to await the arrival of her tow, a large twin-engined tug called the *Utrecht*. After a number of irritating delays, the *Utrecht* slipped her moorings off Sheer-ness and, with her precious cargo, set out on the first leg of a 3,000 mile (4,800 km) voyage across the Atlantic. It took 17 days, arriving on Staten Island, New York, on 22 July, 1975. Now, several years later, the *Peking* has been restored and re-rigged as a static exhibit on Pier 16 on South Street, Manhattan. Next to her lies the *Wavertree*, a 2,118 ton (2,152 t) iron-hulled full rigged ship found languishing as a motor-driven gravel ship in a South American port. Built originally as the *Southgate* in 1885, she has also undergone a long period of restoration. Moored on other piers within the museum complex are a variety of other vessels, rep-resentative of both sail and power of a by-gone era. The *Peking* is open to the public all year round and houses a fascinating col-lection of marine ephemera and artefacts.

Thanks to considerable public interest, a number of maritime historical societies have sprung up in ports around the world. Their interests lie in saving as many of the remain-ing old sailing hulks as possible. Some, like South Street, even have visions of now des-erted quays once more becoming a forest of tall ship masts.

Chapter Five

SAILING SHIP
Decoration

THE ART OF DECORATING *a ship's prow with some form of figurehead stretches back through the centuries. It is generally believed that the custom grew out of a desire to encourage friendly guiding spirits to take up residence during the life of the ship. According to the Bible, the Apostle St Paul made voyages on an Alexandrian vessel which carried a figurehead depicting the deities of Castor and Pollux at her prow. The heads of various sea serpents were carried by some Scandinavian vessels, especially Vikings for whom snorting dragons were a favourite. These were usually removed before entering an unknown harbour or making a landfall, lest the figurehead frighten off friendly land spirits.*

Down the ages, the whims of mariners and their decorative arts have changed along with the fortunes of governments, fashion, superstition and the extent to which a shipowner was prepared to lavish funds on these artefacts. There was usually not much skimping on a warship, but merchant ships have variously been fitted with huge works of art or a matter of fact lump of timber with a few scrolls miserly engraved around the outboard end.

LEFT: *The elaborate and colourful trailboards of the Norwegian sail trainer 'Statsraad Lehmkuhl'.*

ABOVE: *The figurehead and bowsprit complete the aesthetic appeal of a windjammer's curved hull lines. The 'Sagres' makes sail in the English Channel.*

In the seventeenth and eighteenth centuries, the Lion Rampant was a popular choice of figurehead for warships, heavily gilded on English vessels and usually painted red on Dutch ships. Other figureheads included the heads of kings, notable princes, famous warriors from history and horses trampling dragons to death mounted by some famous saint – all worthy subjects for the prow of a new ship. In England, Grinling Gibbons was perhaps the most noted figurehead carver, along with the Hellyers of London who exported their art to North America over a period of more than seven generations.

Artists such as Gibbons made a handsome living out of their carving. In 1598 the cost of the head for the British Navy's *White Bear* was £377. In 1610, the *Royal Prince* decorations cost £1,309; and for another ship of the same name 30 years later the cost had grown to £3,327. The *Sovereign of the Seas,* however, cost a mind boggling £6,691 in 1637! Even allowing that she was the most decorated vessel of her time, the price was outrageous. By 1700, these decorative extravagances had become too

much for the Navy Board who issued the following order:

'Whereas notwithstanding the many cautions which have been given by this Board to the officers of HM Yards against the increasing of HM charge in the ornamental works of HM ships, and the many injunctions to them to use all possible good husbandry therein, several of HM ships are found to have carved works in their cabin coaches and other improper places, which, upon any prospect of action, are torn to pieces by the sailors and consequently a very unnecessary charge; and whereas upon examination of the bills passed for carved work for new ships and ships rebuilt for some time backward, some are thought to be very extravagant and few of a rate observed to agree in charge with another, which renders it absolutely necessary to have some regulation made therein; we have upon mature consideration had thereof thought fit not only to prohibit for the future the putting up of any carved work in the cabin coaches and other

ABOVE: *A cherub, detail from an early figurehead believed to be the work of the 17th century English master carver, Grinling Gibbons.*

improper places of HM ships but also to put a limitation to the charges of the said works by establishing such sums for the several rates and ranks of ships as are not to be exceeded when any of the said ships shall be built or rebuilt viz:–'

During the early 1800s, a small number of ship carvers made a good living working out of small workshops in a number of ports up and down the East Coast of the United States. The trade flourished as ship-owners demanded more elaborate carvings for their magnificent clippers. These ships, because of their fine entry at the bow and the 'clipper' shape of it, needed not only a figurehead, but other carvings along each side of the bow just under the gunwhale. These were called trailboards, and in some cases extended as much as 20 – 30 ft (6 – 9 m) aft of the main carving. Without these additional boards, a magnificent clipper could not possibly look right. The trail-boards, like the figurehead, had become an integral part of the overall aesthetic design.

In addition to the carvings at the bow came the ones at the stern, called the stern

ABOVE: *Detail of the gilded eagle which adorns the bow of the West German ship 'Gorch Fock'.*

LEFT: *Unveiling of the second figurehead carved by Jack Whitehead for the STA schooner 'Sir Winston Churchill'.*

carvings. These were invariably huge, curved slabs of wood with carved ropes depicted around the perimeter with the name of the ship and her port of registry elaborately engraved on the board. Many ships carried them loose, so that they could be shipped aboard for safe keeping when the vessel was at sea. On some ships, the huge figurehead itself was detachable; those which were fixed in place were often carried away in a storm.

England's most famous merchant ship figurehead is undoubtedly that of Nannie the Witch, which adorns the bow of the *Cutty Sark*. The figure is taken from Robert Burns' poem *Tam O'Shanter*. According to the history books, parts of the poem were frequently enacted by the crew of the great clipper as she raced across the oceans. One story goes that they would make a mare's tail by teasing out the strands of a hemp rope and rolling it in old grey paint, and then climb out to the outstretched hand of Nannie and fix the tail in place; there was a strong belief aboard that when Nannie held the tail, the clipper drove faster and harder towards home. A more logical theory is that sailors, being romantic souls at heart, simply thought she looked better with the tail than

ABOVE: The huge gladiator figurehead carved by Norman Gaches for the Bucklers Hard Maritime Museum nears completion in the studio.

RIGHT: Heavily gilded and lengthy trailboards complement the figurehead on the Italian ship 'Amerigo Vespucci'.

without. There are many other such stories, including the one about how the crew would risk life and limb to climb out on the figurehead to place a blindfold around Nannie's eyes whenever a sudden squall appeared approaching from the wrong direction. How much truth there is in these yarns we shall never know, but the fact remains that figureheads were an important part of the ship's furniture and much cared for by the crew.

During one period in the nineteenth century it was fashionable in England to leave the figurehead painted white, with perhaps a little gilding on the raised parts of the trailboards. Elsewhere in Europe, more garish colours closer to those of the painted ladies of the port were used.

Figureheads remained in use on the bows of warships for as long as their shape and the form of construction was suitable for mounting the huge, laminated wooden blocks. The coming of the ram-shaped bow eventually did away with the larger decorations; elaborate escutcheons with supporting decorations appeared in their place, but these too were largely dispensed with by the turn of the century. Merchant shipping continued the custom on some steamships for a while but eventually their owners only gave a passing nod to the idea of decoration by mounting the company badge on the bow, just below the bulwarks.

While the demand for the art of the ship carver is somewhat diminished today, there is still enough work to keep the specialists

ABOVE: *The famous Nannie the Witch figurehead from the 'Cutty Sark'.*

RIGHT: *Detail from the stern carving by Norman Gaches for the brig 'Royalist'.*

LEFT: *Ready for painting; this figurehead for a large yacht by Norman Gaches clearly shows how the yellow pine blocks are at first laminated to obtain the bulk for carving.*

hard at work. Two of the greatest living ships' figurehead carvers, Jack Whitehead and Norman Gaches of the Isle of Wight, have been carving figureheads for nearly 30 years. Their works are now scattered far and wide, sailing on the bows of private yachts, on huge sail training ships, and in the great maritime museums of the world.

Jack Whitehead was an RAF aircraft fitter during World War II and in 1944 his hands were badly damaged in an accident when a propeller backfired. The doctors ordered that he take up some occupation where the muscles in his hands would get constant use. Woodcarving was something he had always wanted to try his hand at and he joined the Lanchester Marionettes – a popular English mini-theatre of the time – carving puppets for their plays of Shaw and Shakespeare. When one of his smaller figureheads,

ABOVE: *Jack Whitehead and his son Michael at work on the massive replacement head for the 'Falls of Clyde'. The figure was carved mainly from a solid block of English elm.*

carved in his own time, found its way to New Zealand on the bows of a yacht, he gave up the theatre and the film industry and directed all his energies to carving ships' figureheads and related artefacts. From the early 1960s he exhibited at the London International Boat Show annually, and on occasion shared a corner of the British stand at the New York Show, subsequently visiting exhibitions in America and Canada.

As commissions came in from all corners of the world, Jack's order book filled up. In addition to carving the heads and trailboards for the twin British schooners. *Malcolm Miller* and *Sir Winston Churchill,* a fascinating collection of figureheads from old windjammers which had been donated to the Cutty Sark Museum in Greenwich, London, were being restored to their former glory by Jack and his wife Doris. Today, this remarkable collection has been installed in the *Cutty Sark* for all to see. His tools are a collection of some 250 assorted chisels, gouges and mallets, many of which are 80 – 100 years old. An adze is used for roughing out figures from huge blocks of

wood which may be anything up to 15 ft (4.5 m) in length and weigh more than a ton (1.016 t) in the raw state.

Norman Gaches, a friend and associate carver who works out of a studio in the coastal town of Ryde, England, has collaborated with Jack Whitehead on a number of occasions. The two men worked on the *Nonsuch,* a replica of the Hudson Bay Company's first ship; the *Golden Hind,* a replica of Sir Francis Drake's famous little ship which made a landfall in San Francisco Bay in 1579; a huge replacement figurehead for the restored warship *Warrior* in the Naval Heritage Museum at Portsmouth, England; and on new figureheads for the training brig *Royalist* and replacements for one or two others which have been lost at sea. The figurehead worn by the *Sir Winston Churchill,* for example, is its second. Norman Gaches carved a magnificent head and trailboards for the training ship *Captain Scott,* built at Buckie, Banffshire, Scotland, eventually renamed *Shabab Oman.*

Another of Norman Gaches' magnificent carvings depicts a huge gladiator, commis-

ABOVE: *A few of the many old figureheads from the collection now on display in the 'Cutty Sark' await restoration at Jack Whitehead's Isle of Wight studios.*

RIGHT: *Ship's figurehead carver Jack Whitehead with a nearly completed figure of Horatio Nelson.*

sioned by the Bucklers Hard Maritime Museum. It now stands proudly at the entrance on a site close to where many magnificent English 'wooden walls' were built and launched into the Beaulieu River on the edge of the New Forest, Hampshire.

One commission which turned into a huge three-year restoration project for Jack Whitehead came when he was asked by the Bishop Museum in Hawaii to carve a replacement figurehead for the *Falls of Clyde*. The original had been lost when the ship was in collision with a steamer in 1913. The figure, of a white lady clutching a rose, was carved from a solid block of English elm weighing 1½ tons (1.5t) and measured 9½ ft (3 m) overall when complete.

Some new figures can take months to complete, as modern glues are the only improvement made on a centuries-old process which in the past required blocks to be scarphed and dowelled together, or held with black iron bolts – a process which caused early rot and the premature demize of many a figurehead. A rough profile outline is drawn on the block with heavy crayon or black paint and the chipping begins. So minutely detailed is the carving on occasion that a 5 ft (1.5 m) figure can take the best part of three months to finish.

LEFT: *Foreign shipowners often used bright colours for their figureheads as seen here on the bows of the 'Christian Radich'.*

A Sailor's Art

CONTRARY TO POPULAR BELIEF, the art of scrimshaw was not prevalent among sailors at large; it was mainly confined to whaleships, where sailors had ample supplies of whalebone on which to practice their craft.

Much more common amongst sailors in merchant fleets was the art of model making, painting and intricate ropework from materials readily available from the locker of a benevolent bosun (boatswain). On a long voyage, and during fine weather spells, a deckhand might find time available between sleeping, eating and keeping a watch to start and finish a model. Many of these were fairly small items carved out of dunnage (timber discarded on the dockside used to stow cargo), the model's rigging and sails being made from odds and ends dropped by the sailmaker whose constant task it was to see that all sails on the ship were patched and repaired.

Many fine models made by seamen are to be seen in maritime museums around the world. Pictured here is an elaborate diaorama of a clipper ship thought to have been made by a deckhand during the 19th century.

The solid block used for the *Falls of Clyde* lady did not begin to take on much shape after several weeks of constant chipping. Work had to stop periodically while other blocks were glued in place to produce additional bulk for the arms, hair, and lengths of flowing skirt which would swirl around the figure's feet. More than a year later, the figure was still not ready for shipping.

As orders are placed with yards around the world for new square riggers, and as restoration projects get under way on headless old hulks, wood carvers are invariably called in to discuss the embellishments. Close examination of the craftsmanship that goes into the making of figureheads reveals what maritime works of art they really are.

Chapter Six

SAIL TRAINING SHIPS
of the World

IN THE SUMMER OF 1989, two very spectacular gatherings of tall ships took place in London, on the River Thames, and at Rouen, France, on the Seine. Both were significant for the huge numbers of ships which managed to sail from many corners of the world to join in the festivities. The programmes organized by the various sail training associations worldwide are not just about sailing and giving youngsters sea experiences of a lifetime; they have become an opportunity for the public to experience at first hand the magical appeal of the ships.

LEFT: *A sight rarely seen in modern times. Square riggers line the quays of the River Seine in Rouen in July 1989. They had come from all corners of the world to take part in 'Les Voiles de la Liberté' ('The Sails of Liberty').*

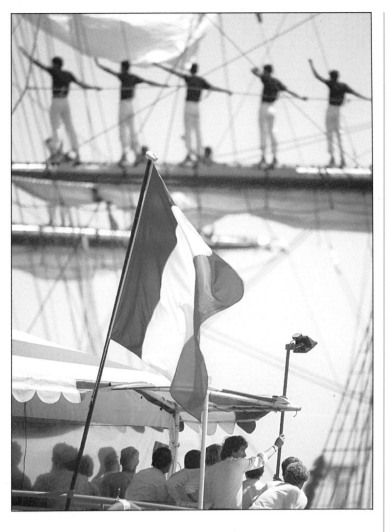

*L*ondon was the starting base for that year's *Cutty Sark Tall Ships Race* which took the entrants out of the Thames, and across the bottom of the North Sea to Hamburg. From there, on Race 2, the ships went to the nearby port of Cuxhaven, up along the west coast of Denmark, and around the Skaw down to Malmo in the south of Sweden; many of them then voyaged on a cruise-in-company to Travemunde. Prior to the start of the race from London, 122 sailing ships of all shapes and sizes were moored along the Thames south of Butler's Wharf, in the Pool of London, off Tower Bridge, and in the old docks further down the river. Many big ships were present, including the largest square riggers in the world – *Kruzenshtern, Mir, Sedov, Alexander Von Humboldt,* and many others. The forest of masts was a sight not seen in the capital for decades and one that is unlikely to be seen ever again; a few miles down river, a new bridge under construction will prevent the larger vessels from navigating to the upper reaches and the heart of the city.

At Rouen, the major outport for Paris on the River Seine, 22 full rigged ships, barques and brigantines, as well as a host of smaller training vessels, were moored along the quay walls in the centre of this famous cathedral city, 75 miles (120 km) from the sea. *Les Voiles de la Liberté* ('Sails of Liberty') had come to help celebrate France's most important anniversary to date, its Bicentennial. These great ships, some of which had slipped away from London to take part, made a magnificent sight and by the time they sailed majestically down the Seine for Honfleur, more than 3 million people had travelled to Rouen to see them.

The sight of a full rigged ship with all canvas set tramping across the ocean is one thing. To be able to see them close up, and to be allowed on board when they are open to the public, is another: their rigs are huge, swathed in ropes and lines that seem to come from all angles. Despite modern technology, many of these vessels still use old-fashioned hemp ropes and Stockholm tar, a

ABOVE: *Performing ballet; sailors man the yards of a tall ship at Rouen while spectactors aboard a tripper's steamer look on.*

LEFT: *The Russian barque 'Kruzenshtern' moored on the Thames River at London. Astern of her is the Polish 'Dar Mlodzeizy' whose slab-faced transom stern can be clearly seen.*

RIGHT: *Crowds of onlookers bustle along the Seine quay at Rouen, France, at dusk as the lights in the rigging of square riggers are switched on.*

black gummy liquid extracted from pine trees which is used to coat rigging, yards, and the hulls of some wooden ships to keep out the weather. The tar's antiseptic, sweet smell permeates the air, wafting over the fleet as a pleasing reminder of voyages made in the dim and distant past.

The Cutty Sark Tall Ships Races began in July 1956, when a fleet of 21 sailing ships from 11 countries raced each other from Torbay, England to Lisbon, Portugal. Most of these vessels were at one time engaged in trading and had recently been converted for sail training, but their future seemed uncertain and the purpose for gathering them together for this event was to celebrate the passing of the age of sail.

Two years later, reinforced by the success of the first event, these ships, joined by a number of others, sailed again. The organizers, The Sailing Training-Ship International Race Committee, recognized that there was indeed a future in adventure training under sail. These gatherings of sail were dubbed 'Tall Ships' by the press, taken

from John Masefield's poem *Sea Fever,* which begins:

'I must down to the sea again, to the lonely sea and the sky,
And all I ask is a tall ship and a star to steer her by'

As race succeeded race, it was clear that these events had more to do with providing adventure and the widening of horizons for young people than paying homage to the past. New square rigged ships were specially built (*Gorch Fock* in 1958, for example) and continue to be built today to provide the opportunity of going to sea for limited periods. The idea is not so much to teach youngsters how to sail a ship, although that is inevitably the case where ships are owned and operated by the various navies; but more to encourage international understanding, to provide the opportunity for youngsters to develop confidence in their own abilities, and nurture team spirit, in an environment free of the constraints of shoreside life.

BELOW: *Cadets on the 'Gorch Fock' stowing tables into the deckhead as the ship prepares for sea.*

To compete in these events, a vessel must satisfy three requirements. Its minimum waterline length must be 30 ft (10 m); half its crew must be between 16 – 25; and its principal means of propulsion must be sail. The Sail Training Association (STA), as it is now known, acquired the first of two 300 ton (305 t) schooners, the *Sir Winston Churchill* in 1966. Two years later, the *Malcolm Miller* followed. Both vessels were designed by Camper & Nicholson and built respectively by Richard Dunston's Haven Shipyard at Hessle and the Aberdeen yard of John Lewis & Sons.

Since 1972, the Tall Ships Races have been sponsored by Cutty Sark Scots Whisky

and are organized annually by the STA and its affiliate, the American Sail Training Association (ASTA). At the end of each race, a major prize is awarded – the Cutty Sark Trophy for International Understanding – to the Master of the vessel which, in the opinion of all Masters of the race fleet, has done the most to promote better international understanding during the race.

The trophy is a valuable silver replica of the clipper *Cutty Sark,* and each member of the winning crew also receives a commemorative medallion. The first holder of this magnificent award was the Russian barque *Kruzenshtern* which received an overwhelming vote in 1974 after taking part in the race from Copenhagen to Gdynia. It was the first year that the USSR had competed in the event.

In 1976, the Belgian 61 ton (62t) ketch *Zenobe Gramme* was awarded the trophy during the race from Tenerife to Bermuda when the skipper of the vessel went to the aid of two smaller vessels which had been drifting on windless seas and were in danger of running out of food and water. Captain Lt George Saille of the *Zenobe* gave up any chance of winning the race and towed the two laggers more than 800 miles (1,280 km) to port.

WINNERS OF
THE CUTTY SARK TROPHY

YEAR	SHIP	COUNTRY
1974	Kruzenshtern	USSR
1976	Zenobe Gramme	Belgium
1978	Gladan	Sweden
1980	Dar Pomorza	Poland
1982	Urania	Netherlands
1984	Sir Winston Churchill	United Kingdom
1986	Atlantica	Sweden
1988	Urania	Netherlands

Another recipient of the trophy was the Polish full rigged ship *Dar Pomorza*. Built in 1909 in Hamburg as the *Prinzess Eitel Friedrich*, she entered every Tall Ships race from 1972, when she won the Cowes to Skagen leg, to 1981, when she was laid up as a museum ship after 72 years of service. Her replacement is the *Dar Mlodziezy*, built between 1981–82 at the Gdansk Shipyard and owned by the Polish Merchant Navy Academy. Shortly after her launch she was able to visit the port of Southampton, in England, for a grand Parade of Sail which took place in the Solent.

A magnificent replacement for her predecessor, the *Dar Mlodziezy* is considerably larger at nearly 3,000 tons (3,048 t). She carries a crew of 38 plus about 140 cadets and measures 357½ ft (109 m) overall. Her rig is that of a full rigged ship and is easily recognized by her somewhat unusual flat transom. A number of labour saving devices are installed on board; modern winches hoist the sails and brace the yards; and her yards are fixed on modern lightweight, pole masts, obviating the need for their raising and lowering when sail is set or taken in.

The Cutty Sark Trophy, awarded to the ship deemed to have done most towards international understanding during the Tall Ships Races.

ABOVE: *The Sail Training Association's topsail schooner 'Sir Winston Churchill' disappears behind a wave in the English Channel as she heads south on one of the annual Cutty Sark Tall Ships Races.*

RIGHT: *The Norwegian sail training ship 'Christian Radich' casts an early morning reflection over Milbay docks.*

ABOVE: *The Polish square rigger 'Dar Pomorza' under sail off the Isle of Wight. She is now a museum ship and has been replaced by the 'Dar Mlodzeizy'.*

LEFT: *A blaze of lights from the rigging of square riggers celebrating 'Les Voiles de la Liberté' at Rouen in 1989.*

The Russian three master *Druzhba* was built in 1987 and is the same size as the *Dar Mlodziezy*. She is based in Odessa, but like all of the big Russian ships, will compete in the annual events wherever they may take place. South and Pan American countries such as Argentina, Uruguay, Chile, Columbia, Venezuela and Mexico are also keen supporters of the annual STA events. In 1979, the Venezuelan government launched the *Simon Bolivar,* the first of a generation of new windjammers. She is a barque measuring 270 ft (82 m) overall, and was built at Bilbao in Spain, her distinctive grey and black paintwork giving her a fine appearance despite her flat transom.

The same yard of Astilleros y Talleres Celaya, Bilbao, built the Mexican Navy's *Cuauhtemoc* a little longer and with the more traditional counter stern. She carries nearly 25,000 sq ft (7,620 sq m) of sail and is manned by a crew of 275 officers and sailors. She carries the name of an early Aztec emperor who was taken prisoner and executed in 1525 under the orders of the Spanish *conquistador* Hernan Cortes.

One of the most unusual square riggers to have been built in recent years is the British barque *Lord Nelson* which was launched in 1983 for the Jubilee Sailing Trust. This vessel measures 163 ft (49 m) and was designed by the eminent naval architect Colin Mudie especially to cater for the needs of the handicapped. Wide and uncluttered decks allow room for manouevering wheelchairs, and special lifts and hoists are installed to allow the handicapped to take an active part in the running of the ship.

A new 193½ ft (59 m) topsail schooner has recently been launched and fitted out at the Damen Shipyard at Gorinchem in Holland for the owners Het Zeilende Zeeschip. *Eendracht,* which means 'unity', replaced an earlier and much smaller two masted schooner of the same name, and accommodates a regular crew of 13 with about 40 extra trainees. The steel hull is fitted with a 550 horsepower (40 kW) diesel engine and her rig carries about 3,445 sq ft (1,050

sq m) horsepower of sail. The Het Zeilende Zeeschip Foundation is operated along similar lines to the British STA, as are many other organizations which have been established around the world.

Poland, like the USSR, gives great encouragement to sail training programmes. The Iron Shackle Foundation was established to give youngsters not in the services

BELOW: *The Polish ship 'Dar Mlodzeizy', her sails neatly furled on their yards, is nudged alongside the quay at Southampton, England.*

the opportunity to go sailing. The *Pogoria,* built in 1980 at the Gdansk Shipyard, is a three masted barquentine of 342 tons (347 t) measuring 154 ft (47 m) overall. She has a regular crew of 20 and can carry 36 trainees. Four interlinked shackles, the emblem of the fraternity, are depicted on each of the ship's five square sails.

ABOVE: *The Russian training ship 'Druzhba' sails down the River Seine. Her contemporary hull lines and modern deck fixtures are clearly visible in this picture. Note the enclosed lifeboats slung in modern gravity davits.*

When Australia celebrated her Bicentenary in 1987, Great Britain's gift to the country was a purpose-built schooner called *Young Endeavour*. Her rig is actually a cross between that of a topsail schooner and barquentine. She carries a staysail and a loose footed spanker between the fore and mainmast, as well as a fore course, and lower and upper topsails on the foremast. A gaff rigged main and topsail is carried on the mainmast. The 115 ft (35 m) vessel was built at a cost of almost £1 million ($1.6 million) by Brooke Yachts at Lowestoft and sailed on her maiden voyage to Australia as part of the 'First Fleet' re-enactment. Twelve of her crew were young Australians selected from more than 7,000 applicants, and it is hoped that she will remain in service for at least 50 years, giving a possible 60,000 youngsters the opportunity to taste life at sea.

Steel is still the most popular building material for these ships, even small ones such as the 76 ft (23 m) brig *Royalist*, built at Cowes in 1971 for the United Kingdom Sea Cadet Association. Steel is easier and less costly to maintain than timber, which after a few season's hard use generally requires careful and labour-intensive maintenance to keep it in top condition. Once in a while, however, wood is still used. The Irish Sail Training Committee's *Asgard II* was built in 1981 to a design which had been drawn up almost 30 years prior to her launch. Rigged as a brigantine, the *Asgard II* measures 84 ft (25.5 m) overall and has a distinctive green painted hull.

In the mid 1950s, when the first reunion of the world's remaining seaworthy sailing vessels took place off Torbay, few would

have dared to predict that within a few decades the world's tall ships fleet would number in the hundreds. As the beginning of a new century rises over the horizon mariners will be able to look back at 150 years of sophisticated sailing rig development, the demize of one era of commercial sail, and the beginning of another which spawned both restoration of the old and construction of new vessels for training purposes. The time is rapidly approaching when a number of vessels launched in the early part of the twentieth century will have to be retired. Such is the enthusiasm and support of the public and some governments for the various organizations in Europe, the Americas, and more recently in the Antipodes, that replacements for these older ladies of the oceans will continue to roll down the slipways. The gradual growth in the size of these fleets, the increasing cost of oil to run conventional motor ships, and the environmental stand on nuclear power has also rekindled the hope of a number of ship designers that sail can still be a commercial success, even if in limited areas.

TOP RIGHT: The Australian barquentine 'Leeuwin' creates a glorious sight as she sails across a glittering Indian Ocean.

BOTTOM RIGHT: The Danish wooden hulled three master 'Elinor' leans to the breeze as she and the modern Polish training ship 'Pogoria' sail down Southampton Water.

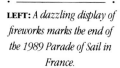

LEFT: A dazzling display of fireworks marks the end of the 1989 Parade of Sail in France.

Chapter Seven

SAILING INTO THE
Twenty-First Century

FOR MORE THAN A DECADE AND A HALF, nautical engineers and naval architects in many countries of the world have been looking at ways to reduce the dependency of merchant shipping fleets on oil as their prime source of energy. In Japan, a research team at one of the world's largest shipbuilders, Nippon Kokan (NKK), first tackled the problem in 1977 and concluded that a ship driven by wind power alone would be too costly to run.

A 3,000 ton (3,048 t) windjammer requires a crew of 60 – 86 if a part cargo, part cadet training scheme is operated; without cadets, a crew of 30 – 40 would still be required, and that allowing for modern winch gear and other labour saving devices being installed. Compared with the 20 or so crew needed to operate a modern 200,000 dwt super-tanker, the figures for a larger sailing vessel would obviously not be viable.

LEFT: *Modern tall ships 'Wind Spirit' and 'Wind Star' sail in company. Rigged as staysail schooners, the ships' sails are controlled by an on-board computer.*

high as 50% by one source, but this was subsequently revized by the NKK team to a 10% saving being directly attributable to sail power, the balance being shared by improved hull, engine and propeller design. NKK's ultimate plan was to build a 20,000 ton (20,320 t) ship fitted with three 130 ft (39.5 m) tall steel masts on which would be rigged reinforced plastic-made sails. The vessel would be used to transport cars to the West Coast of North America. Other smaller ships were also planned for short haul coastal trading.

In England, Walker Wingsail Systems of Plymouth have been working on a variety of 'wingsail' powered projects since the late 1960s. Their prototype, 'Planesail', was a trimaran hull on which was mounted a single mast supporting a number of vertical wingfoil sections. The whole mast could be rotated relative to the angle of wind to drive and control the vessel. In recent years, the basic principle behind this early project has been retained for a number of commercial applications, the most successful of which was the fairly recent fitting of a Walker Wingsail unit to the m.v. (motor vessel) *Ashington*.

The Walker Module 2 wing thrust unit was mounted atop the vessel's funnel on a free running vertical axis bearing. It was linked to two control computers, one of which was fixed to the thrust unit where it monitored wind speed, direction and the ship's course, adjusting the flaps and control tail according to software parameters stored in its memory.

In practice, the m.v. *Ashington*'s Master reported improvements in fuel saving, in the movement of the ship in a seaway, in providing a reliable back-up in the event of main engine failure, in assisting with docking and reducing costs for tuggage, and in a significant reduction in wear and tear on the main engine components. Following their two-year experiment with the Walker unit, the owners de-rigged the vessel, claiming that while it had proved partly successful, there were contributing factors

ABOVE: *The Walker Wingsail unit in place on the motor vessel 'Ashington' owned by Stephenson Clarke.*

RIGHT: *A view along the upper deck of one of the three Windstar Sail Cruise ships clearly showing the simple staysail rig. Lightweight alloy extrusions are used for the masts and spreaders, with automatic roller reefing on the jib sails. Engine exhausts are blown clear of the sails by the specially shaped funnel.*

*H*owever, NKK researchers came up with a kind of hybrid vessel. A small model of a sailing motor ship was put through wind tunnel tests and eventually an 80 ton (81 t) working version called the *Daioh* was built and put to sea in the Bay of Nagoya. Equipped with three mainsails and a 15 horsepower outboard motor, the *Daioh* was crammed with instruments for measuring the effectiveness of sail design. The results were so encouraging that NKK pressed ahead with a larger design. The 1,600 dwt tanker *Shin Aitoku Maru* was fitted with masts on which rotating rigid wingsails were mounted; these were controlled by an onboard computer programmed to regulate engine output in proportion to wind velocity. Initial claims on fuel saving were put as

ABOVE: *The French aluminium hulled schooner 'Club Mediterranee' was, at 236 ft (72 m) overall, the largest sailing ship to be sailed single handed across the Atlantic.*

TOP: *A schooner dips her lee rail under in heavy weather on passage to Green Island in the West Indies.*

which prohibited the unit achieving a high success rate, namely that the routes operated by this size of vessel were too short, and in areas where winds tended to blow in fickle fashion; and that the equipment required considerable experience from the crew and ship's master to obtain the best performance; a problem exacerbated by frequent changes of Master and crew.

Some of the most important research done on commercial sail has been that carried out by the W. German firm Prolss and Wagner in association with the Institut fur Schiffbau of Hamburg, and which has been continued in recent years by the Dynaship Corporations of Denmark and the United States. The work was begun originally in 1957 by the engineer Wilhelm Prolss, whose aim was to design a wind powered commercial vessel that could successfully compete with motor driven ships of the period.

Once again, the major operational cost savings were made in the manning levels and the result was a fully automated vessel

ABOVE: *'Wind Spirit', a modern windjammer rigged as a staysail schooner, can cruise at 8 knots in a moderate breeze. She is equipped with hydraulic winches and derricktype booms for convenient sail handling.*

had to be done on stability before further progress could be made. And none of these commercial designs to date retain the aesthetic appeal of the original square rigged vessels.

Some progress has been made in the area of schooner rigs, however, following the building of two large yachts for single handed racing in the 1970s. Both *Vendredi Treize* and *Club Mediterranee* were designed to compete in *The Observer* newspaper's sponsored single handed transatlantic race known as the OSTAR, which raced from Plymouth, in Devon, across the Atlantic to Newport, in Rhode Island.

The rules of the race at this time encouraged the building of larger yachts and in its simplified form, one aspect of the theory of hull design effectively states that the longer the waterline length of the vessel, the faster its natural hull speed. In 1972, Frenchman Jean Yves Terlain entered the 128 ft (39 m) *Vendredi Treize* for that year's OSTAR. The yacht was designed by American Dick Carter who began the design project by first drawing the largest possible rig which could be easily handled by one man and then designing a hull to fit it!

Vendredi was fitted with three masts and given Carter's Luna rig, which is much like a staysail rig, but each sail has a larger area and reaches from deck to masthead, with the clew sheeted. Tacking is relatively simple with the rig generating about 70% efficiency. Terlain finished in second position behind his rival and fellow countryman Alain Colas, who sailed a trimaran.

Colas was a dedicated yachtsman obsessed with establishing himself as the world's premier single handed sailor. After being defeated in a subsequent race around Great Britain in 1974 in the same trimaran he had sailed across the Atlantic, and later around the world in record time, Colas began to think in terms of a larger yacht for the next OSTAR, in 1976. After seeing the potential of *Vendredi* four years earlier, he set out to design and build the largest vessel ever sailed single handed.

which linked an on-board computer fed with weather predictions to rigging control equipment capable of rotating mast sections and controlling the amount of sail set. The rig itself comprized a number of cylindrical masts which could be rotated through 180°. Six aerodynamically curved yards would be fixed to each mast, on which lightweight terylene sails would hang from and be attached to travellers, rather like curtain rails, at the head and foot. The proposed 16,000 ton (16,256 t) Dynaship would have been fitted with six such masts supporting some 30 sails to give a total sail area of well over 100,000 sq ft (30,480 sq m). The effects of wind pressure on a vessel of this size so rigged would be enormous, and wind tunnel testing showed that much more work

RIGHT: *Display of the on-board computer monitor on 'Wind Star' which allows officers on watch to finely tune the ship's sails.*

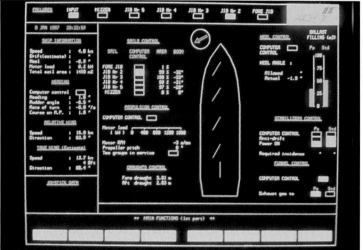

ABOVE: *The modern cargo-carrying staysail schooner 'Atlantic Clipper' under way in the Solent shortly after her commissioning in 1984.*

By dint of sheer commercial enterprize, the Frenchman raised the not inconsiderable sum of money needed to build his dream boat. *Club Mediterranee* was the result. At 236 ft (72 m) overall, she had a theoretical speed potential of 20 knots, which would surely be more than enough in a race comprized largely of smaller craft to beat the pants off the nearest rival, *Vendredi* – by now renamed *ITT Oceanic*.

Club Mediterranee was a four masted Bermudan staysail schooner built of aluminium, and in her racing mode, was packed with electronics. In fact, her equipment was so exotic that the race committee that year ruled that Colas could not use his satellite navigational equipment, his weather fax, or his radar. The main on-board computer was a Wang 2200 desk top for which special software had been developed that would

Club Mediterranee is a large yacht (the *Cutty Sark* is only 212½ ft (65 m)) and has now undergone a complete refit to transform her into a working charter yacht offering sailing adventures with a difference. Inspired by her performance over the years, Windstar Sail Cruises launched a brand new ship in 1986 that was recognized as one of the most imaginative projects to set sail in the cruising market for decades.

Wind Star and her sister ships, *Wind Song* and *Wind Spirit* are each 440 ft (134 m) long, rigged as four masted staysail schooners with masts rising some 204 ft (62 m) above the waterline. Sail setting, furling, and sheeting is controlled by an on-board computer linked to hydraulically operated winches controlled from the ship's bridge. The computer monitor also gives the officer of the watch a clear indication of wind speed and direction relative to the ship's speed, course and position, so that minute adjustments can be made to the rig to achieve the most efficient result.

These ships are breaking new ground in a largely untapped sector of the tourist trade, but they are not just a novelty designed to draw custom. Each vessel has an efficient sailing rig which performs well in open waters where winds are fairly predictable, allowing a relaxed cruising pace to be achieved with quite substantial savings in fuel costs to the operator.

These new ships are not unlike designs drawn by American naval architect Hugh Lawrence for a Bermudan rigged staysail schooner of 4,000 tons (4,064 t) in 1976. His marine laboratory tests based on the actual log of an earlier windjammer, *Fennia*, wrecked while rounding the Horn in the 1920s, were carefully monitored by a symposium of naval architects, shipping economists and engineers who gathered in London. Their express purpose was to investigate the numerous alternatives put forward for a return to cargo-carrying sailing ships.

Until it can be proved that it is practical to sail large ships of the type currently opera-

allow the skipper to monitor every part of the rig and the ship, providing instant read-outs from 14 different stations. The computer also monitored the ship's solar, wind and water generators as well as the on-board diesel powered unit which provided the power for all the electronics.

In spite of all the sophistication, Alain Colas was beaten by rival French yachtsman Eric Tabarly, sailing the much smaller 63 ft (19 m) ketch *Pen Duick VI*. Colas's yacht suffered a number of rig failures in severe gales as he battered his way across the Atlantic, failures which eventually forced him to put into Newfoundland for repairs. His predicted 18 day crossing, which might have proved possible had conditions been just right, was stretched to 24.

ABOVE: *Modern yacht sheet winches and Dutch halyard winches are used on 'Atlantic Clipper' to control the sails.*

FOLLOWING PAGE: *'Atlantic Clipper' uses auxiliary engines linked to a hydraulically-driven propeller to keep her moving in calm conditions.*

ting on trade routes, it is unlikely that we shall see ships of this size converted or even designed and built for the transportation of cargoes under sail. Nonetheless, there are routes on which they could operate, where fresh winds can be guaranteed for up to 70% of the time, and smaller vessels used on short haul coastal or inter-island routes have great potential.

Atlantic Clipper was purpose-built to operate a transatlantic cargo route from Plymouth, England, to islands in the Caribbean. At 220 tons (223.5 t), she was probably the first commercial sailing ship venture built for more than 50 years and cost almost £250,000 ($400,000). Launched in 1984, the vessel measures 108 ft (33 m) overall and can sail at 10 knots or more when loaded with 100 tons (101.5 t) of cargo. *Atlantic Clipper* is rigged as a staysail wishbone ketch with hand-operated monster sheet winches similar to those found on a large yacht. The main halyard winches for hoisting sail are similar to old fashioned types found on trading barges manufactured by Strikwerda of Schaard in Holland.

A unique feature of the vessel is her twin Perkins diesel engines housed in a steel compartment on deck, well above the waterline. Her twin variable pitch propellers are driven by hydraulic pumps which can also be utilized through a switchover valve chest to operate the vessel's own cargo derricks used for loading and discharge. Under sail, the *Atlantic Clipper* can average 5–6 knots in a moderate Force 3–4 breeze and 9–10 knots in stronger winds.

As the quest for alternative fuels continues, it will be difficult for ship designers to ignore the wealth of historical facts relating to sail power. There are areas of marine commerce where sail power has proved to be effective. Where design and construction can be linked with knowledge gained from the aeronautics industry and professional yacht racing to use lightweight fabrics and construction materials, special ships will continue to be launched with sailing rigs as shipowners bid to harness the wind.

WHERE TO SEE THE TALL SHIPS

THE STA (SAIL TRAINING ASSOCIATION) organizes races for each year. In 1991, the race will start from Milford Haven in Wales. Participants will gather there between July 11th and 14th and sail to Cork, Republic of Ireland, for a parade of sail taking place between July 16th and 20th. The next port of arrival will be Belfast, Northern Ireland, where the fleet will visit between July 23rd and 27th, before setting off for Aberdeen, Scotland, and then finally on to Delfzijl in Holland, where they are due to arrive between 13th and 17th August.

The following year will see one of the largest gatherings of Tall Ships so far at Cadiz, Spain, where a fleet will gather from feeder races starting in Lisbon and Genoa from April onwards. Called the 'Grand Regatta Columbus', the fleet will participate in the quincentenary celebrations of Columbus' voyage of discovery to the New World and will sail from Cadiz to The Canary Islands, before voyaging onward across the Atlantic to San Juan in Puerto Rico, northward to New York and Boston on America's east coast, and then east across the North Atlantic to Liverpool, where they are expected to arrive in August.

SAIL IN A TALL SHIP

THE SAIL TRAINING ASSOCIATION of Great Britain, in addition to offering berths for the 16–24 year-old group, also runs 'Management Training' voyages. Private individuals aged between 21 and 69 can apply to join certain voyages on the schooners *Sir Winston Churchill* and her sister ship *Malcolm Miller,* which are sailed during the months of February, March, May, September and November.

Contact the STA, for information, at:
5 Mumby Road, Gosport, Hants, PO12 1AA, England.

For further information on other organizations offering berths for charter, contact:

The Association of Sea Training Organisations,
c/o The Royal Yachting Association, RYA House,
Romsey Road, Eastleigh, Hants, SO5 4YA, England.

The American Sail Training Association,
PO Box 1459, Newport, RI 02840, USA.

GLOSSARY

ABACK: terminology used by sailors when the wind is on the forward face of a sail. 'Caught aback' describes a sudden wind shift likely to stop a vessel from sailing forward. Yards and sails are often trimmed deliberately to put the wind on the fore side of a sail to help manoeuvering.

ABAFT: towards the stern. Aft of a vessel's widest point, its beam.

ABEAM: at right angles to the fore and aft centre-line of a vessel.

ALOFT: in the rigging, towards the upper yards, 'in the tops'.

ANCHOR: drop forged iron implement attached to a ship by a length of chain which, when lowered to the sea-bed, secures the vessel in a fixed position.

AUGER: hand tool for boring holes in timber, used in sailing ship construction.

BALE: goods like wool were wrapped in burlap and secured with rope or wire.

BALLAST: pig-iron (small brick shaped lumps of cast iron), scrap iron, gravel, stones, sand; any heavy substance which could be placed low down in the ship's hold to help keep the ship stable when the cargo was light or non-existent.

BATTEN DOWN: to secure the loose hatch covers over each hold with tarpaulins and wedges. Usually the carpenter's job.

BELAYING PIN: a bar of iron with one moulded end to fit the hand used to secure a rope, usually halyards, and found in the pin rail or rack at the base of each mast.

BINNACLE: the brass case which houses and protects the compass. An integral kerosene lamp was lit at night to allow the helmsman to steer. Large iron balls either side of the compass can be adjusted to correct the compass.

ABOVE: *The Norwegian sail trainer 'Christian Radich' under way in the English Channel.*

RIGHT: *More than 3 million people flocked to see 'Les Voiles de la Liberté' moored at Rouen on the River Seine in 1989.*

BITTS: large timber posts set through the deck, or metal bollards bolted through the deck, used to secure the moooring ropes (or warps) when berthing.

BLOCK: pulley (sheave) mounted between two wooden parts (the shell) used to increase the mechanical power of ropes, particularly running rigging. Blocks are made with single pulley wheels, double, triple and sometimes more, and are frequently used in pairs.

BOOM: spar along which the foot of the sail is stretched. It is secured to the spar at the tack, or heel, and the clew, the outer bottom corner of the sail.

BOWSPRIT: spar projecting from the prow of a vessel to which are secured the forestays. These standing parts of the rigging help to stay the foremast in position, while the bobstay, of rope or chain, leads from the bowsprit end to the stem of the ship and secures the bowsprit against the tension of the forestays. The forestays are used to carry the foresails.

BRACE: a rope which is rove through a block, secured to the yard end, used to trim the yards to the wind.

BULWARKS: a rail of solid plate or wood planking, of waist height or higher, which effectively raises the freeboard of the vessel and helps to keep water off the maindeck.

BUNK: (also called a berth) a sailor's bed. A fixed piece of furniture fitted with removable bunk boards, secured in place in heavy weather to prevent the occupant from being thrown out as the ship pitched and rolled.

CAPSTAN: usually fixed on the fo'c'sle head, this is a revolving barrel which used to be rotated by hand using spokes fitted in the capstan head and used for raising the anchor before the days of chain.

CATHEAD: a short boom on older vessels on which the anchor was secured after being raised from the deep before being stowed. On clipper ships and windjammers, the cathead remains, and has become a part of the carved decorations at the prow of a vessel.

CHAIN: (also called cable); made of drop-forged iron in open and stud link. It is made in lengths and secured together with large shackles. Each length in a large merchant ship measures approximately 90 ft (27 m) or 15 fathoms.

CHAIN LOCKER: a space under the fo'c'sle head where the anchor chain is stowed.

CLEAT: a wood or metal device secured through the decking or on a mast, with short outstretched arms around which ropes and warps are secured in a figure of eight fashion.

CLEW: lower corners of a square sail, outer lower corner of a triangular sail or any sail which is rigged in fore and aft fashion.

DAVIT: a steel or iron post with its top part curved, from which was slung a block and tackle used to hoist the fluked end of the anchor so that it could be stowed. Generally, any small crane like device on a rotating

ABOVE: *The brig 'Astrid', with the race yacht 'Steinlager II' in the background.*

BELOW: *A pulling gig aboard the Italian 'Amerigo Vespucci'. Note the ornate gilded stern carvings.*

mount at the side of the deck which can be used to heave pieces of equipment aboard.

DEADWEIGHT: the maximum capacity of a ship measured in tons. Includes cargo, stores, passengers, crew and fresh water.

DISPLACEMENT: the amount of liquid displaced by any vessel measured in tons.

DORY: flat-bottomed boat used by the long-line fishermen of the Newfoundland Grand Banks which were carried on deck to the fishing grounds by the mother ship schooner.

DRAUGHT: measurement from the bottom of a ship to the water level at which the vessel floats. A variable measurement in merchant vessels read from marks on the hull at the stem and stern and used to calculate the vessel's displacement.

FAIRLEAD: a device fitted to the bulwark or at the edge of the deck through which a rope is passed to give it a fair lead to its tying off point.

FENDER: in the past, a device made of coir rope, stuffed with rope ends (fag ends), used to protect the ship's side from grazing a dock wall. Nowadays, any fabric, rubber or inflatable device used for the same purpose.

FREEBOARD: measurement of the part of the vessel's hull which is out of the water, taken from the water level to the upper deck.

GALLEY: the kitchen.

HATCH: an opening in the deck through which cargo is loaded.

HAWSE PIPES: tubes fixed at an angle from the foredeck through the side of the hull at the forward end through which the anchor chain runs. The chain is fed from the chain locker, up to the deck through a spurling pipe, over the windlass and out through the hawse pipe.

HEADS: a ship's w.c. This was located on a grating over the beak-head in the forepart of the vessel.

HEEL: lower end of a mast.

HELM: generally a wheel linked to machinery used to control the rudder.

HOLD: cargo space.

HOOPS: bands of wood used on a fore and aft sail to attach it to the mast. Also made in iron and sweated over a spar to give it extra strength.

JIB: triangular fore and aft sail set on a fore-stay in front of the foremast, secured on the bowsprit or stemhead and hoisted aloft by halyard.

JIBBOOM: spar which extends from the bowsprit on which fore and aft sails (jibs) can be set.

JURY RIG: emergency sailing rig set up from anything to hand after the main rig has collapsed, blown away or suffered dismasting.

LAMP LOCKER: space allocated for the stowage and care of oil burning ship's lights.

MAIN COURSE: mainsail. The largest sail set on lowest yard of the mainmast.

MAIN DECK: principal deck, the working deck. In older sailing ships, the uppermost watertight deck running the full length of the ship.

MATE: Captain's chief officer next in line of command.

MESS ROOM: space allocated to the crew for taking meals. Not always located next to the galley. In some sailing vessels, meals were carried along the main deck to the fo'c'sle, often being served cold.

RIGHT: *Sailors manning the yards to loose the sails aboard the 'Simon Bolivar'.*

BELOW: *The 'Belem' during France's 1989 Bicentennial celebrations, sailing down the River Seine.*

MONKEY RAIL: a rail fixed above but running parallel to the bulwarks on the quarterdeck.

MOONSAIL: fine weather sail set above skysails.

PAINTER: light rope fastened to the bow or stem head of ship's boat, used for making the craft secure.

PIN RAIL: special fabricated steel rail or length of timber with holes into which are slotted belaying pins for tying off sheets, halyards and warps. Commonly found under bulwark rails and at the base of each mast.

PLATES: sheets of rolled steel or iron riveted to frames used to fabricate the hull, decks and superstructure of a ship. Modern ships use welded plates.

POOP: the raised portion of the deck at the stern from where a sailing vessel was steered. Apart from seamen on helm duty, only officers of the watch and the captain were permitted on this deck.

PORT HOLE: circular window made of cast bronze fitted with strengthened glass, located in the hull and superstructure. In heavy weather, a hinged bronze plate attached to the outer ring is lowered and secured over the glass to prevent the ingress of water.

RUNNING RIGGING: down hauls, clew lines, braces, jack stays, footropes, sheets, mast ropes, top tackle, and a host of other adjustable lines used to control the hoisting and set of sails, the angle of yards and the raising and lowering of upper masts and spars, are collectively called 'running rigging' or 'running gear'.

SAMSON POST: a single post of substantial dimensions fitted through the deck of small craft and secured on a bulkhead or at the keel, used for mooring the vessel.

SCUPPER: also called a 'wash port'. An opening, with a hinged plate, fitted in the bulwarks on the main deck which allows water to run off the deck.

SEAM: the joint between planks in a ship's side running fore and aft. To ensure watertight integrity, the seam is filled with oakum banged in tight with a caulking iron. Pitch or marine glue is used to cover the seam.

SKYLIGHT: deck windows in opening frames set in raised coamings, usually of teak, opened from below. The captain's day room in many sailing ships was usually fitted with a large skylight, its windows opened by winding gear.

SPANKER: fore and aft sail set on the mizzen mast. The head of the sail is supported by a gaff and the foot by a boom.

SPLICE: a method of joining two ropes, a broken rope or wire ropes by interweaving strands of the respective parts into the other. A rope's strength is weakened by splicing, but can be improved by using a long splice instead of a short one.

STANDING RIGGING: masts are supported in four directions, from forward by 'stays', from aft by 'back-stays' and from each side by 'shrouds'. In a sailing ship these parts are secured when the masts are set-up and only adjusted during annual refits.

SUPERSTRUCTURE: a structure built on and fixed to the upper main deck, ie a wheelhouse, galley, passenger accommodation.

TABERNACLE: a three-sided steel or timber casing secured to the deck into which a mast is stepped. The spar can be held in place by a steel pin running transversely

through the tabernacle and mast, or by a steel shoe at the heel of the mast. The device allows the mast to be easily raised and lowered.

TACK: term used when a vessel changes direction whilst turning to windward, ie when it moves through the eye of the wind from starboard tack to port, or vice versa. Also, bottom fore corner of a fore and aft sail.

TOPSIDES: that part of the ship clear of the marked water-line.

TRUCK: the plate-shaped wooden cap fitted to the mast top, also called a button, hence the expression 'truck to keel'.

WAY: a vessel is said to be carrying 'way' when it is moving through the water; 'under way', 'sternway', etc.

WELL DECK: a part of the upper deck enclosed between 'islands' of superstructure.

WINDLASS: apparatus for raising and lowering the anchor.

WINDWARD: the 'windward side' is the side from which the wind is blowing ('To windward' etc).

YARD: a spar hung across a mast used to carry sail. Can be trimmed to the best angle to take advantage of the wind.

YARD ARM: outer part of the yard.

ABOVE: *The 'Cutty Sark' seen in dry dock at Greenwich, London.*

RIGHT: *Dawn breaks west of the Azores as the 'Peking' is towed across the Atlantic.*

INDEX

BIBLIOGRAPHY

HISTORY OF SHIPS, partworks, Ian Allan. SHIPS MONTHLY
   magazine, various issues, Waterway Productions Ltd.
THE CLIPPER SHIPS, Time Life Books Inc, 1980.
THE WINDJAMMERS, Time Life Books Inc, 1980.
MEN, SHIPS & THE SEA, National Geographic Society, 1973.
THE ROMANCE OF THE CLIPPER SHIPS, Basil Lubbock, Hennel
   Locke Ltd, 1948 (in association with Seven Seas Fine
   Arts, London, 1945).
DISASTER LOG OF SHIPS, Jim Gibbs, Superior Publishing Co,
   1971.
THE VISUAL ENCYCLOPEDIA OF NAUTICAL TERMS UNDER SAIL,
   Trewin Copplestone Publishing Ltd, 1978.

SHIPWRECK, Jonathan Cape Ltd, 1974.
GRAIN RACE, Eric Newby, George Allen & Unwin Ltd, 1968.
GREAT YACHTS AND THEIR DESIGNERS, Jonathan Eastland,
   Rizzoli, New York, 1987.
I REMEMBER THE TALL SHIPS, Frank Brookesmith, Seafarer
   Books, 1980.
THE SET OF THE SAILS, Alan Villiers, Pan Books Ltd, 1955.
SEAFARING AMERICA, Alexander Laing, American Heritage
   Publishing Co Inc, 1974.
SINGLE HANDED, Ebury Press, 1984.